Great Sporting
Trivia

The Five Mile Press

The Five Mile Press
22 Summit Road
Noble Park Victoria 3174
Australia
Phone: +61 3 9790 5000
Fax: +61 3 9790 6888
Email: publishing@fivemile.com.au

First published 2002

Editor: Sonya Plowman
Cartoons: Geoff Hocking
Cover Design: Sonia Dixon
Design: SBR Productions, Olinda, Victoria

Printed in Australia by Griffin Press

National Library of Australia
Cataloguing-in-Production data

Ross, John.
Great sporting trivia

ISBN 1 86503 604 8.

1. Sports – Miscellanea. I. Title
796.02

Great Sporting
Trivia

John Ross

The Five Mile Press

Contents

Introduction   7

The Old Days of Sport   11

Sporting Dramas and Disasters   61

Heroes of the Sporting World   101

A Cavalcade of Characters   149

Weird Tales from the World
    of Sport   191

The Wide World of Sport   251

Conversion Tables   288

Why do we love trivia, especially sporting trivia? What do we find so appealing about the story of the footballer who had only one AFL match and one kick to win the Grand Final, or the Olympic runner who stopped to conduct a band – and still won? Or the man who was expelled from his club, and so he built one of the world's great sporting clubs?

Well, humans are inquisitive creatures – but also, regrettably, lazy. When it comes to absorbing information we can't be bothered starting at A and working through to Z, but would much rather let all sorts of haphazard facts wash over us, allowing the most interesting bits to stick in our brains, according to taste. And the quirkier the facts, the more fascinating they are!

We invented sport because we're also intensely competitive. When the first caveman threw a rock at a passing beast the ancient sport of shot-putting had its beginnings. Spears followed, then bows and arrows and all that aiming stuff! When the first cave-woman outran her club-swinging mate we were into the running sort of sports.

These were purely survival skills until the Greeks started running around with no clothes on at the early Olympics. Discus-throwing, chariot racing, wrestling and leaping were added to the range of fun things to do. Then somewhere along the way someone kicked a ball, someone hit a ball, and someone discovered that if you hit a ball with a stick it might (just might) go further than if you threw it.

We've come all this way to the modern world of sport – which obsesses us and keeps us sane through all the stress and strain of living. To balance out the general angst, there's the pure joy of sport. We love to play it, reserving special places in our lives for that game of football, tennis, basketball, or just for a run around.

We follow our teams and our favourites, working ourselves into a blessed fever pitch at matches. We watch sport endlessly on television, listen to it on radio – and pity our forebears who either had to be at the game or rely on secondhand news.

We read about sport endlessly and forever. Have you noticed how the sports sections of the newspapers are expanding, while the news seems to be shrinking? We're living in our perfect sporting age. But, that is just today's news. What about the whole panoply of world sport and all those arcane pieces of sports history that we love to soak up?

What about those weird events and coincidences, the crazy things some people do, the characters and the master sports people of other times and places? What about the baseballer who was so fast that it was said he could turn out the light and be in bed before the room got dark? What about the best soccer team in the world, built around just one man? What about the jumps jockey who rode in 48 races and had 49 falls? And why *did* those Greeks run in the nude?

Great Sporting Trivia takes you there. Ah, sports trivia buffs, this book is for you. You can read it for five minutes, or five hours. You can read little stories or long ones. You can roam the world of sport, being a part of thousands of sporting moments!

Now, read on!

John Ross, 2001

Chapter 1

The Old Days of Sport

All the McLeans

The McLean family was outstanding in Rugby Union. Its scion Douglas McLean played three Tests for Australia in 1904/5. His son Alexander toured South Africa in 1933 and played against New Zealand in 1934 and 1936. His brother William was selected for the 1939 Wallaby tour, which played no games because of the War. He captained the Australian team to New Zealand in 1946 and the 1947 team to Britain and Europe. Jack McLean was a member of the 1946 Australian tour, but played no Tests. William's brother Bob had two sons, Paul and Jeffrey, who both represented Australia, Jeff in 13 Tests and Paul in 31 Tests, in which he became Australia's leading points scorer. William's son Peter, known as Spider because of his lean build, played 13 Wallaby Tests. The McLean stand at the Ballymore Oval in Brisbane honours the family.

Back in Harness

An absence of players in the Essendon team against Collingwood forced the secretary of the club, William Crebbin, to play his first game in five seasons in 1900.

Baseball Beginnings

The game of baseball descended from the English game of rounders, and was being played in various forms in America in the eighteenth century. Organised sport was started by the Knickerbocker Club of New York in 1842, and the basic rules were created in 1845, and remain essentially the same today. Baseball spread out from this New York base and by 1859 California had a club. By 1871, 10 clubs formed a professional association, the oldest professional club being the Cincinatti Red Stockings, which had toured the country in 1869. By this time baseball was already being referred to as America's national game.

★★

Bats and Balls

Cricket was played in Australia from the time of the arrival of the First Fleet, which had some bats and balls in the cargo. The first recorded match took place in 1803 according to a report in the official government paper the *Sydney Gazette and NSW Advertiser*. The report said that 'the late intense weather has been very favourable to the amateurs of cricket'. The match reported took place on the Sydney Domain. The Australian Cricket Club was formed in 1926. Most early cricket clubs took place around public houses, and gambling was a normal part of the proceedings. Many early clubs expired, but the Melbourne Cricket Club, formed in 1838, only three years after settlement of the Port Phillip district, survived to become the most powerful club in Australia.

★★

Big British Tour

Just as an Aboriginal team was the first Australian team to play cricket in England, a 'New Zealand Native' team was the first to take Antipodean rugby back to the Motherland. The team, the brainchild of English businessman John Eyton, consisted of 20 Maoris and four Europeans. The reason for the four Eupopeans was that Eyton had trouble making up the numbers of Maoris, so he invited four dark-haired players who could pass for Maoris to join the squad. The team played a total of 107 matches in 14 months, winning 78 of them. It first went to Melbourne, where it played some Australian Rules matches. After the tour of Britain, 14 games were held in Australia and a further eight in New Zealand. The players had such a good time they were reluctant to break up when they got back to home base in Auckland.

Big Deal

Hugh D. McIntosh was known as Huge Deal McIntosh because of his entrepreneurial flare. In Sydney at the turn of the century he started his career by selling pies at racetracks, but graduated to staging prize fights and refereed the world heavyweight championship at Rushcutters Bay between Jack Johnson and Tommy Burns. McIntosh bought the

Tivoli Circuit of Vaudeville Theatres and owned the *Sunday Times* newspaper. He opened a chain of milk bars in England, but his business failures began to outweigh his successes and he died penniless in London in 1942 at the age of 68.

★★

Bowling Along

Ten-pin bowling derived from a form of bowling conceived in Germany, which was originally a religious ceremony. A churchgoer would roll a stone down the isle of the church to knock down a club called 'the heathen'. If he succeeded, it proved his faith. The game went to America and was played in the Plymouth Colony as early as 1621 with Dutch colonists enjoying a game of skittles called nine-pins. In 1920, 10-pin bowling began in New York City. The sport was commonly associated with drinking and gambling and the bowling alleys were usually next to a tavern. In 1850 New York City had an estimated 400 bowling alleys.

★★

Big Throw

The betting theme in early cricket surfaced when Australia went to England in 1882 and the gigantic Australian batsman George Bonnor wagered fellow passengers on the *SS Assam* that he could throw a cricket ball more than 100 yards. Upon landing at Plymouth a ground gathered at a nearby barracks where Bonnor threw the ball 104 yards and won 100 sovereigns. Bonnor's big hitting and statuesque appearance were drawcards in these early Test matches. His prowess was evident in a match in 1885 against England, when he made 100 in 100 minutes and 128 in 115 minutes with 4 fives (there were no sixes in those days) and 14 fours.

★★

Boxing's Beginnings

Fist fighting is as old as man himself, but according to boxing historian Nat Fleischer, the first authentic fight or contest in America, where rules were laid down if not wholly observed, took place in 1816 when Jacob Hyer beat Tom Beasley and claimed the American heavyweight championship. No one challenged him and he never fought again. The number of bouts increased continuously in the nineteenth century with Tom Hyer, the son of Jacob, beating 'Country' McCloskey in 101 rounds on 9 September 1841. Tom Hyer was also acclaimed American heavyweight champion. Fighting was associated with gambling powers and taverns and was frowned upon by authorities. Christopher Lilly and Thomas McCoy fought for 120 rounds near Yonkers, New York, in 1842. McCoy died after being hit by 81 punches in the final round. Boxing prospered to the point that the Olympic Club of New Orleans in 1890 had John L. Sullivan, a bar room brawler who had never been beaten, defending his heavyweight title against 'Gentleman' Jim Corbett for $25,000. Corbett knocked out Sullivan in the twenty-first round.

★★

Brilliant Ballarat

Football talent was more evenly spread in the early days, so much so that an all-star team from the Victorian Football League was thrashed by Ballarat when it visited in 1897. Ballarat won 13.11 to 8.6.

Crazy Leap of Faith

A mediaeval monk named Elmer is said to have used an elementary form of hang-glider to fly from the top of Malmsbury Abbey in Wiltshire, England. The first modern pioneer of hang-gliding was Otto Lilienthal in Germany in the 1890s. Modern hang-gliding has now become both a sport and a recreation with national and world championships occurring, particularly in Britain and the United States. Connected with hang-gliding is the development of microlight aircraft. These were originally hang-gliders with motors attached. The idea was that the motor could be stopped once the desired altitude had been reached and the gliding mode could then take over. Today's microlights are purpose-built aircraft with a flex wing similar to that of a hang-glider – with a tricycle unit attached for take-off and landing.

Crimson Flash

Queenslander Arthur Postle, who was known as 'the crimson flash' because of the colour of his running singlet, was virtually unbeatable up to 75 yards and in 1906 set a world record for 75 yards at 7.2 seconds at Kalgoorlie. On the same day he defeated his opponent Irishman Bernard Oday at 130 yards and 300 yards. Postle competed in both Britain and South Africa and he was acclaimed world sprint champion in 1910.

Cruising Cavills

The Cavill family of Sydney made a remarkable impact on swimming in Australia. Father Fred Cavill came to Australia from England in 1879 and leased the Lavender Bay Baths where he conducted Learn to Swim classes. Of his nine children, several were to become internationals. Ernest Cavill was the 1000 yards champion of New South Wales. Dick 'Splash' Cavill was the first Australian to swim 100 yards in under a minute. Sidney Cavill won the Australian 220 yards championship, and Percy Cavill won the world five mile championship. Charles Cavill was the first to swim the entrance of San Francisco Harbour while Arthur T. Cavill won both Australian amateur and professional sprint titles.

★★

Demon Bowler

An early Australian Test cricket star was Fred Spofforth, a fast-medium bowler who was known for his accuracy and his wonderful yorkers. Spofforth toured England five times with Australian teams and took 94 wickets in Tests. His two greatest performances were in 1879 when he took 13/110 against Lord Harris's team, including a hat trick, and in the famous Ashes Test at The Oval in 1882. He took 7/46 in the first innings and followed it with 7/44 in the second.

Double Sided

In its early days the Melbourne Cricket Ground had an ingenious grandstand that could be turned around so that cricket could be watched on the oval in the summer season and football in the park outside during the winter. The stand burned down.

Early Games Events

As the ancient Olympics developed, the most popular events became boxing, wrestling and a combination of both called the Pankration. Other popular events were the tethrippon, a four-horse chariot race and the pentathlon, which included a sprint, long jump, discus throw, javelin throw and wrestling.

Early Games

Hyde Park was the first sports ground in Australia. It was planned in October 1810 by Governor Macquarie as the area for recreation and amusement. It became a popular venue for horse racing, but cricket, hurling, quoits and rugby were also played there.

Fighting Tiger

Australian spin bowler Bill O'Reilly was nicknamed Tiger and he certainly exemplified this in his attitude to bowling. He bowled at a slow-medium pace and relied on variations in pace and length and a bouncing 'bosie', or 'wrong un', which was virtually undetectable. Batsmen suffered great strain in facing him, as he was naggingly accurate and always aggressive in his approach to bowling. After a Test career of only 27 Tests, with 144 wickets, he retired and later become a forthright and popular writer on the game as well as a successful businessman.

First Car Race

Auto racing began in 1894 with a race of about 78 miles from Paris, France, to Rouen. Two years later there was a 54 mile race in Chicago, which was won by Frank Duryea, who averaged 7.5 miles an hour while driving through a snow storm.

★★

First Class

The opening first-class cricket match that took place in Australia was between Van Diemen's Land (Tasmania) and Victoria. It followed a challenge issued by the Melbourne Cricket Club to the Launceston Cricket Club in 1850. The match did not take place until February 1851, and then it was staged as part of the celebrations for their newly independent colony of Victoria. The Victorian team sailed to Launceston aboard the *SS Shamrock* and appeared on the field at the Launceston Racecourse wearing the red, white and blue colours that the MCC team still wears today. The first ball bowled was an underarm delivery by William Chitty of Tasmania to Duncan Cooper of Victoria. The match was won by Tasmania with scores of 82 and 37. Preparations were immediately made for a return match in Melbourne with the party of nine Tasmanians crossing Bass Strait in February 1952. Three Melbourne-based competitors from Launceston completed the Tasmanian team. The game was played on the then MCC Ground on the south bank of the Yarra. This time Victoria won with scores of 80 and 127. The deciding third match was played a year later and Tasmania won easily by eight wickets.

★★

First for Fanny

Fanny Durack was the first female swimmer to win a gold medal in the Olympics when she won the 100 metre freestyle in Stockholm in 1912. She set 12 world records and one time held every world record in women's swimming for 50 yards to one mile. Although she retired in 1921, she did not compete in any other Olympic contests.

First Olympian

Edwin Flack was Australia's first Olympic champion. Flack came from Melbourne where his father had opened an accountancy practice. Flack was sent to England for further experience and his father arranged for a job for Edwin with his old firm Price Waterhouse. Flack decided to travel in 1896 to the Olympic Games in Athens after having some experience in running with athletic clubs in London. His idea in going to the Games was that he would try to compete, but if not would enjoy being a spectator. Flack's first race on the opening day was the 800 metres and he finished well ahead of the field. Before the final, he lined up on the second day in the 1500 metres and won it in 4 minutes, 33.2 seconds. He was the first non-American to win in any track and field event at the Games. The third day, Flack teamed up with his English friend

George Robinson in the doubles in lawn tennis and they won a bronze medal, although Flack was beaten in the first round of the singles. Eventually Flack lined up in the 800 metre final and won it against three other runners in 2 minutes and 11 seconds. As soon as that was over he drove off as he was intent in running the first Olympic marathon, although he had never run a race longer than 10 miles. The effort was too much for Flack and while a companion ran off to get a blanket to put around him, he asked a Greek bystander to support him. The Greek hugged Flack and he took exception to this attention and punched him. He was then loaded into a carriage and driven to the stadium. He later became a senior partner in his father's firm and died in Melbourne in 1935 aged 62.

Five Clubs Enough

Leonora Wray had a remarkable career in the early years of women's golf in Australia. She won her first major title in 1906 with a mere five clubs, and won the National Title in the next two years. She then contracted typhoid fever and did not play for 10 years, but came back to win the Australian Title again in 1929. She was still going strong in 1950 when she captained and managed the Australian Women's Golf Team to England.

★★

Gentleman in Gloves

Bert Oldfield was a long-serving Australian wicketkeeper, playing in every Test from 1921 to 1937. He was known as 'the gentleman in gloves' because of his modest demeanour and restrained appeals. He stumped 52 of his 130 Test victims, an international record, helped by the fact that he was keeping 'up' to Bert Oldfield, Clarrie Grimmett and Arthur Mailey. Oldfield owned a sports store in Sydney and he kept in form by insisting that his staff members never pass anything to him, but throw objects to him so he could catch them. His career was bracketed by two World Wars and he served in both of them.

Gentleman Jack

Jack Crawford was known as one of the world's most stylish tennis players and was always impeccably turned out in his long cream trousers as he played on the world circuit. From Albury, New South Wales, Crawford was not of the upper classes, but he had the demeanour of grandeur on the court and was a favourite of the Queen (now the Queen Mother) when he won Wimbledon in 1933. That year he also won the French and Australian Opens, but the grand slam eluded him when Fred Perry of America beat him at Forrest Hills, New York.

Golf Course Master

Dr Alistair McKenzie was a master of golf course design and he left his mark in Australia with some of the most magnificent golf courses the world has seen. In Melbourne he designed the Royal Melbourne, Kingston Heath and Victoria Golf Clubs, which are part of the famous sand belt area. He also made the original designs for the Royal Sydney Golf Club, the Australian Golf Club, the New South Wales Golf Club, the Royal Adelaide Golf Club and the Royal Queensland Golf Club. McKenzie's courses are distinctive for their characteristic of having been carved out of wild terrain. His use of gorse and stands of trees as backdrops adds special character to his rolling fairways and generous bunkering.

Honourable Captain

One of Australia's most honourable, if not most successful, captains was Harry Scott, who led the Australians on a tour of England in 1886. Weighed down by the cares of captaincy, he decided to stay in London and further his studies in medicine. Scott was a graduate of Melbourne University and played for St Kilda and East Melbourne, combining his medical duties with his cricket career. He made a Test century at The Oval during the 1884 tour of England. His habit of seeing London on bus tours, which cost him tuppence, earned him the nickname Tup. He became a respected country doctor and Mayor of Scone in New South Wales and said about the 1886 tour: 'I have captained Australia. I have hit a Test century. Many would have liked two such honours such as these.' He died of typhoid in 1910 at the age of 52.

Jack of All

Harold Hardwick won victories in two wildly different sports when he was part of an Australasian team of 10 which was sent to the 1911 Festival of Empire in London, staged to commemorate the coronation of King George V. Hardwick won the 100 metre swimming and was then approached by the team manager to ask if he would compete in the heavyweight boxing championship. Hardwick had boxed against the famous Australian middleweight Les Darcy and done quite well. After some quick sparring practice, he beat William Hazel, the English titleholder, so badly that the referee stopped the bout after only two and a half minutes. An hour later Hardwick fought Canadian Julius Thompson in the final, and won again in just 2 minutes, 30 seconds. The next year of the Stockholm Olympics, Hardwick avoided the boxing ring and won the gold medal in the 4 x 200 yards freestyle relay and two bronze medals in swimming.

Jockey Mourned

Tommy Corrigan was a famous and popular jockey of early days. He came with his family from Ireland and settled near Warrnambool and won the first VRC Grand National Hurdle in 1881. With his flamboyant manner and huge moustache, Corrigan was an enormous favourite with crowds and there was great grief in 1894 when he was killed when his mount Waiter fell during the Caulfield Grand National Steeple. The funeral held four days later showed his popularity as the long route from his house in Caulfield to the Melbourne General

Cemetery, a one and a half hour journey, was lined with people who came to pay their respects. The cortege consisted of an assembly of jockeys on foot, a large number of horsemen and 240 carriages.

Jockey Out to It

Jockey Bill Evans collapsed after winning the Melbourne Cup on Apologue in 1907, and was weighed-in by being laid unconscious on the scales with his saddle on his chest. He had fasted severely for the race, wrapping himself in whisky-soaked towels, and did not have the strength at the end to lift his cap to the crowd. He recovered about an hour later.

Journeyman Dan

Dan Minogue is the only Australian Rules footballer to have had playing and coaching involvement with six clubs. He joined Collingwood in 1914 before joining the army. He came back to captain-coach Richmond and then coached another four clubs: Hawthorn, Carlton, St Kilda and Fitzroy.

Long Kicker

St Kilda star Dave McNamara thrilled the crowd at Collingwood in 1923 with three enormous kicks from defence. One was from 75 yards, another of 84 yards and a shot that missed the goal was measured at 93 yards. McNamara said long kicking was easy, but he said it was impossible to kick more than 100 yards, presumably disputing earlier claims for a 100 yard kick by Essendon's Albert 'The Great' Thurgood.

★★

Longest Kick

The longest kick in AFL football is reputed to have been made by Essendon player Albert Thurgood in 1899. The distance of 107 yards, 2 feet was measured by astounded Essendon officials after he produced the place kick at training.

★★

Loud Mouth

The barracking of Yabba was a highlight of cricket matches at the Sydney Cricket Ground in the 1920s and 1930s. With his gravel voice and humour, Yabba's comments from the Sydney Hill became legendary. Yabba was a Balmain rabbit-seller. His real name was Stephen Gascoigen. His comments like 'Get a bag' and 'Have a go you mug' were expanded to statements like 'Bowl him a piano and see if he can play that.' When bodyline Captain Douglas Jardine waved a fly away, he called out, 'Hey Jardine, leave our flies alone.' When an umpire rose a hand to a side board attendant who appeared to be asleep, he called, 'It's no use umpire, it'll have to wait till play time like the rest of us.' The great English batsman, Jack Hobbs showed his appreciation of Yabba's comments when, on his last appearance at the Sydney Cricket Ground, he walked over to the fence and shook his hand.

Marathon Hero

The modern Olympics gained a home-grown hero at Athens in 1896, when Spiridon Louis, a 24-year-old shepherd from Amarousion, won the marathon, a race created to honour Pheidippides, the messenger of Marathon in 490 BC.

Men Only

Originally the ancient Olympics were for men only, but eventually women were allowed to compete. The first female athlete champion was Kyniska of Sparta, who won the tethrippon in 396 BC and repeated the victory in 392 BC.

Modern Women

The first women to compete in the modern Olympics were Madame Brohy and Madame Ohnier of France, in the croquet event of 1900 in Paris. Charlotte Cooper of Great Britian was the first woman champion, in tennis.

★★

Naked Runners

The original Olympic runners wore a loincloth, but when Orsippus of Megara ran naked and won, nudity became the standard.

Name Changes

In Australian Football League, clubs had strange nicknames in their early days. Carlton was known as the Old Dark Navy Blues while Essendon was known as The Same Olds from a team song, which said 'we are the same old Essendon'. Fitzroy was originally known as the Maroons but became known as the Gorillas before the Lion's emblem was successfully introduced in 1957. Footscray was originally known as the Tricolours but it was dubbed the Bulldogs after a genuine bulldog led the players out in 1928. Geelong was known as the Pivotonians, as the city was once described at the Pivot of Victoria. The Cat emblem was introduced in 1923. Hawthorn was known as the Mayblooms and for a time the Mustard Pots for its brown and yellow colours but Roy Cazaly, the coach, introduced the Hawks in 1942. Melbourne has gone from the Fuchsias, named after the red and blue colours of the bush, and the Redlegs until it was described as the Demons by coach Checker Hughes in 1933. North Melbourne were the Shinboners, possibly originating from local butchers decorating their display windows with beef bones in blue and white colours. Richmond was the Yellow and Black Angels and also the Wasps before it became the Tigers. St Kilda went from the Seagulls to the Panthers and then to the Saints, while South Melbourne were known as the Southerners, the Bloods or the Blood Stained Angels before becoming the Swans. Only Collingwood has retained its original name of the Magpies, named for the large numbers of magpies that frequented the banks of the Yarra near the Victoria Park ground, and also for the black and white colours of the club.

★★

New York Ban

Boxing was banned in New York for 10 years from 1910, but it was well and truly back by 1921 when Jack Dempsey fought Georges Carpentier of France in the first fight, with $1 million gate receipts. This was held at Madison Square Garden, a luxury venue that had transformed boxing into a society night out, with the men wearing tuxedos and the ladies in evening finery. That was followed by a $2 million gate for a fight between Dempsey and Gene Tunney in 1927.

Old Bowlers

The ancient Egyptians are believed to have played a game similar to lawn bowls at around 5200 BC but the earliest recorded bowling green is at Southampton at 1299. The modern rules for bowls were drawn up in Scotland in 1948-1949 by Glasgow solicitor, William Mitchell. The English Bowling Association was founded in 1903 with Test cricketer Dr W. G. Grace as its first president.

One Hundred Up

The centenary of AFL football was celebrated at the MCG on 7 August 1958 when Scotch College and Melbourne Grammar students donned old-style clothes to play in a re-enactment of the famous first match in 1858. The match, which was on and off over a period of three days, ended in a scoreless draw. It is commemorated in a statue outside the Melbourne Cricket Ground. Australian Rules Football was codified and organised before two of the most important sports in the world, Rugby Union football and soccer, became organised. However, the game partly derived from the schoolboy game of rugby, experienced by its founder Tom Wills.

Our Oppy

Hubert Opperman was a cycling champion in the 1920s. At the age of 18, Oppy became Australia's greatest long distance, city-to-city record breaker and at one stage held every major Australian record and some world track records. His ride from Perth to Sydney via Melbourne and Canberra was not surpassed for 32 years. Opperman won the Paris-Brest-Paris non-stop classic and was the first Australian to finish in the Tour De France. Opperman later had a successful business career and went into politics, becoming minister for immigration. He was still cycling every day.

Our Walter

Melbourne billiards player Walter Lindrum was a phenomenon – as dominant in his sport as Don Bradman was in cricket. He was official world champion from 1933 to 1950 and established more than 50 records, including a world record break of 4137. The son of Australian billiards champion Fred Lindrum, young Walter became a professional player at the age of 12. Although right-handed in everything else, he played billiards left-handed. He was so brilliant that the rules of billiards had to be altered to curb his massive scoring, with his favourite 'nursery canon' being outlawed. Despite this, he continued to break world records. Lindrum was a tireless worker for charities and was awarded both the MBE and the OBE.

Over the Barrels

A popular ice-skating sport of the nineteenth century, barrel jumping, was revived in America in the 1950s. The object is to jump over a series of barrels lying on their sides, with barrels added after a round of jumps have been completed. The person with the longest jump wins. North American and US Championships are held every year.

Perfect Swallow

Sydney-born Dick Eve is the only Australian to have won a gold medal in an Olympic diving event. Eve won the men's plain high tower diving at Paris in 1924, by the simple method of executing one perfect swallow dive, which gained a maximum of 10 points from the judges.

★★

Pistol Packers

Americans John and Sumner Paine became the first brothers to finish first and second in an Olympic event, in the 1896 military revolver-shooting event.

Players Start New Code

The breakaway game of Rugby League started when 22 clubs formed in England to create their own competition – after the Rugby Union officials refused permission for players of northern clubs to receive payments for loss of wages. So the more elite Rugby Union game continued to flourish among their amateurs in the south of England, while the tough game of League flourished in the north. The League clubs first met at the George Hotel in Huddersfield in 1895 to form the Northern Union. The number of players per side was reduced from 15 to 13 and the Union changed its name in 1922 to the Northern Rugby League. Rugby Union is traditionally said to have had its beginnings at Rugby, a famous public school, when during a game of scrum football in 1823 William Webb Ellis picked up the ball and ran with it. The new handling code of football developed and was played at Cambridge in 1839.

Popular Support

When Carlton vice-captain Harry Downs was rubbed out for kicking in 1931 and suspended for two seasons, 1800 Carlton members packed an angry meeting at the Brunswick town hall to protest and thousands of witnesses were prepared to say that Downs was innocent. His suspension stood.

Road Race Classic

The Melbourne to Warrnambool cycling classic is the toughest road race in Australia. It originated in 1895 when riders started the 260 kilometre trek from Warrnambool to Melbourne and the winner completed the journey in 11 hours and 44 minutes, having received a two hour start from the scratch men who clocked 10 hours and 52 minutes. The handicap event now has a race record established in 1980 at five hours and 37 minutes and 10 seconds. Former winners of the event are famous Australian cyclists such as Hubert Opperman, Russell Mockridge and Peter Besanko.

Scheme Goes Wrong

Bribery in cricket goes as far back as 1881, when three members of the visiting English team were alleged to have been offered bribes to be non-triers in a match against Victoria. The alleged scheme failed when Victoria made an unexpected collapse in the second innings and gave England a win. It was alleged that two players, George Ulyett and John Selby, were to receive £500 each if Victoria won and William Scotton, £250. Selby made a remark to Scotton after the match which disclosed the bribe, but Ulyett threatened him to be silent or he would 'jowl your heads together'. Ulyett and Selby also assaulted Billy Midwinter, who refused to be part of the scheme and reported it. One of the players who was not in the scheme, Ted Peate, who took 6/30 in Victoria's disastrous second innings, said the bookmakers were very badly hit by the result of the match. 'Certain of their schemes failed, much to the satisfaction to most of us,' he said. The *Australasian* newspaper said: 'Professional cricketers who keep late hours, make bets to some amount and are seen drinking champagne at a late hour with members of the betting ring when they ought to be in bed, must not be surprised if people put a wrong construction on their conduct.'

★★

Sea Bathing

The prudish laws about sea bathing which existed early in the twentieth century were challenged in 1902 by the proprietor and editor of the *Manly and North Sydney News*, William Gocher. Gocher bathed during daylight hours at Manly, thus defying the law, but police refused to prosecute and the law became obsolete. The right to bathe in public view was won. Before Gocher's stand bathing boxes on wheels were trundled into the sea so that women could step in to the water to protect their privacy.

★★

Serial Winner

The most successful athlete of the ancient Olympics was Leonida of Rhodes, who won 12 championships between 164 BC and 162 BC.

Showgirl

Annette Kellerman had a remarkable career in swimming and in showmanship. She was introduced to swimming as a child as a means of strengthening her legs and by the age of 16 had won two state titles. In 1905, she followed with her father to Europe to promote a professional swimming career. She made three unsuccessful attempts to swim the English Channel and then was on stage for a season at the London Hippodrome. She went to the United States in 1906 and gained fame in Vaudeville but was arrested on a Boston Beach for wearing a skimpy one-piece bathing costume. Throughout her career she continued to swim in movie stunts and made some spectacular swimming feats. After a varied career in America she returned to Australia in 1970.

Soccer Grows

The English Football League was the brainchild of William McGregor of Aston Villa who called the first meeting of interested clubs to the Andersons Hotel in Fleet Street, London on 22 March 1888. The first formal meeting took place and a month later on 17 April at the Royal Hotel, Manchester, and 12 members agreed to form the football league. The first football league clubs were Bolton Wanderers, Everton, Preston North End, Stoke City, Wolverhampton, Wanderers, Derby County, Accrington, Burnley, West Bromwich-Albion, Aston Villa, Blackburn Rovers and Notts County.

Steeplechaser

One of Australia's best-known poets, Adam Lindsay Gordon, was a great horseman. Sent to South Australia to curb his wild behaviour, he became a policeman and then a politician, and also began publishing his sporting verse, which was collected into *Bush Ballads and Galloping Rhymes*. An inheritance enabled him to indulge his passion for horses and steeplechasing. He rode three steeple-chase winners in one day at Flemington, Victoria, in 1868, an unsurpassed feat. After a decline in fortune, injuries from race falls and melancholia exacerbated by the death of his daughter he took his own life at the age of 37.

Sydney Fight

The big heavyweight title fights moved to Australia in 1909 when Jack Johnson became the first black American to win the heavyweight championship, by knocking out Tommy Burns in the fourteenth round in Sydney. The fight created a search for a 'Great White Hope' who could beat Johnson and he was finally beaten in 1915.

The Big Match

The highlight of the Football Association year is the FA Cup, a knockout competition open to all divisions. The biggest win in the FA Cup occurred in 1887 when Preston North End defeated Hyde United in the first round, 26 to nil. The biggest final win was by Bury over Derby County, 6-0 in 1903.

The First Games

The ancient Olympic Games were held every four years in the valley of Olympia, south-western Greece, starting in about 776 BC. The Games opened with the lighting of a flame at the Altar of the god Zeus. The Games were mostly religious observance, and the only athletic event was the stadion, a sprint over about 200 metres. The first winner was Koroibos, a cook from Elis. Originally the runners wore loincloths but after Orsippus of Megara ran naked and won, nudity became the standard. The last Games of the ancient Olympics took place in AD 393 when they were abolished by the Emperor Theodosius of Rome, who considered them to be a pagan ritual. After lasting more than 1100 years it would be another 1500 before the Olympic Games were revived.

The Hardy Scots

Shinty is an exclusive Scottish game played by 12 a side, using a curved stick known as a caman to propel a ball with a thick leather covering about the size of a tennis ball. The game has its antecedents in the ancient game of camanachd, which means 'sport of the curved stick'. It was brought to Scotland from Ireland by Celtic emigrants in around the fourth century. The sport is thought to be a substitute for training for battles between clans, and the matches are fierce and hotly contested.

★★

The Human Buzzsaw

Henry Armstrong, one of the greatest American boxers, had such a relentless fighting style that he was know to fans by such nicknames as ' Hammering Henry', 'Homicide Hank', 'the human buzzsaw' and 'perpetual motion'. From Mississippi, he won the world featherweight, lightweight and welterweight titles all in one year, 1937. He had 174 professional fights and won 145 of them, 98 by knockouts.

The Oldest Race

The Stawell Gift is the world's oldest professional foot race and one of the premier sporting events in Australia. It was first run in 1878 for a £24 first prize which was won by farmer W. Millard. The Gift meeting has been held annually over the Easter weekend except for the Second World War. The race was run over 130 yards until 1973 when the distance was changed to 120 metres. The Stawell Gift is always held at precisely 3.15 p.m. and has never been postponed.

The Pieman

William Frances King became known as the flying pieman in Sydney when, between 1842 and 1851, he specialised in bizarre walking and running feats. His efforts included walking 1634 miles in 39 days, 1000 quarter miles in 1000 quarter hours, six miles in one hour, four minutes and four seconds, and one and a half miles in 12 minutes carrying a 40 kilogram goat. He twice beat the mail coach from Sydney to Windsor. He was known as the pie man as he owned a street stall selling pies and was one of Sydney's colourful street characters.

★★

The Terror

The record of Charles 'Terror' Turner in taking 106 wickets in the 1887/1888 Australian season has never been surpassed, nor has his 283 wickets on an overseas tour in 1888. To get those figures he played in 36 matches, which would be unthinkable with the short tours of today. 'Terror' Turner was the other part of an outstanding bowling combination with Fred 'The Demon' Spofforth. English batsman Turner bowled at a lively medium pace, was very accurate and spiced his bowling with off breaks and leg cutters. He took 678 wickets on three tours to England. On Spofforth's retirement he formed an equally deadly combination with the left arm spinner J. J. Ferris.

The Visitors

The first match between a team from England and one from Australia took place at the Melbourne Cricket Ground on New Years Day, 1862. The Englishmen were captained by H. H. Stephenson, captain of Surrey, who brought out a party gathered from the best England professional players of their day. A crowd of around 15,000 to 25,000 Melbournians turned out on a very hot day to watch the historic encounter. The teams were of 11 Englishmen against 18 Victorians, with their team colours displayed in ribbons on their sun hats and similarly coloured sashes for their waists. The English tour was sponsored by Melbourne hoteliers Felix Spiers and Christopher Pond. They had originally tried to bring the novelist Charles Dickens to Australia for a lecture tour and when he failed to reply they decided to bring out a cricket team instead. The first international ball was bowled by Billy Caffyn to Melbourne publican and footballer Jerry Bryant. Victoria made 118 in the first innings while England made 305 and then bowled the Victorians out for 92. A total of 45,000 people watched the match and enjoyed the entertainment, refreshments from Spiers Pond's tents and diversions such as a balloon ascent, the first in Australia. The takings for this one match in Melbourne covered the expenses of the entrepreneurs for the whole tour. The team played other matches against Victoria, Geelong, Sydney, Bathurst, Ballarat and Bendigo. Spiers and Pond made an enormous profit of £11,000, which was invested in railway refreshment rooms in England and the Criterion Hotel in London, to add to the holdings of Spiers and Pond in Australia of the Royal Hotel and the Cafe De Paris. One of the players from England summarised the tour by saying of the Australian cricketers: 'Well I don't think much of their play but they're a fine lot of drinking men.'

★★

Tiny Decima

Decima Norman was tiny in stature but a phenomenally good sprinter. She was unable to participate in the 1936 Olympics, despite times superior to other athletes, because her state of Western Australia did not have an official athletics association. The association was formed in 1937 and she was selected for the 1938 British Empire Games in which she won a record five events: the 100 and 220 yards, the long jump and as a member of the 440 and 660 yards relays. She moved to Sydney to prepare for the 1940 Olympics, which were never held because of the war.

Top Wrestler

Milos of Kroton won the boy's wrestling championships in the Ancient Olympics in 540 BC, and later won the senior title five times straight. He was defeated in the final in 512 BC by Timasetheos of Kroton.

Trick Shots

Joe Kirkwood was a trick shot golfer. Although he held records on several Australian courses and won the Australian PGA and Open Championships, he earned more money from his exhibitions of trick shots. One of his stunts was to put three balls on top of each other on the tee and drive the middle ball down the fairway without touching the other two balls. He would also have an attractive girl hold a golf ball on a tee in her mouth and hit the ball without disturbing either the tee or the precious teeth of his assistant. He nicknamed his twin sons Pitch and Putt.

★★

Unlucky Suburbs

When Footscray, Hawthorn and North Melbourne were admitted to the VFL in 1925, suburbs which missed out in their bids were Brighton, Brunswick, Camberwell, Caulfield and Prahran.

Unsafe Crowds

Crowd safety was of little concern to officials in the early days of sport, and particularly with massive crowds at some events standing on grandstand roofs, sitting on guttering, hogging the aisles and spilling out onto the grounds. At the small Richmond ground it was quite common for the wooden perimeter fence to be smashed down from the press of the crowd in the outer. In 1920, Princes Park was overflowing with almost 50,000 people when Carlton and Collingwood played for a place in the Four. The same number went to the small South Melbourne ground in 1923 for the 'Lake Premiership' between South Melbourne and St Kilda, again to decide a place in the Four. They covered the grandstand roof and spilled over the fence to the very edge of the boundary line. Added attractions were St Kilda's Dave McNamara, the champion forward, and South Melbourne's Roy Cazaly, master ruckman.

★★

Very Pukka Game

Badminton originated as a game called *poona* in India, where it was discovered by British army officers and taken to England. In 1873 the Duke of Beaufort played it with friends at his country place, Badminton, and so it became known by that name.

World Beaters

The 1924-25 All Blacks were the first New Zealand Rugby Union team to go through a tour of England unbeaten. They played 32 matches for 32 wins in England, Wales, Ireland, France and British Columbia, scoring 836 points and allowing only 116 to be scored against them. The greatest victory came against England at Twickenham, at a time when England regarded itself as the powerful home of the game. Early in the game one of the All Black forwards, Cyril Brownlie, was ordered off for allegedly kicking another man. New Zealand had conceded the first try, but they were so enraged by what they saw as an injustice that they overpowered England. None was angrier than Brownlie's brother, Maurice. The big forward helped create a try with one of his strong charges, and then powered over the line himself, carrying England players over the line with him.

Women Allowed

The ancient Olympics were for men only at first, but women were eventually allowed to compete. The first female Olympic champion was Kyniska of Sparta, who won the tethrippon, a four-horse chariot race, in 396 BC, and again in 392 BC.

★★

Women's Cricket

The first women's cricket match was recorded at Gosden Common in Surrey, England, in 1745. The first woman's club was the White Header Club founded in Yorkshire in 1887 and the first women's Test match was played between England and Australia at Brisbane in December 1934. The highest individual score in women's cricket was 190 by Sandra Ugawhal for India against England in 1986. The best bowling figures have been 7/6 by Mary Dugan for England versus Australia in 1958 and 7/7 by Betty Wilson for Australia in the same series. Betty Wilson's analysis also included the only Test hat trick.

Chapter 2

Sporting Dramas and Disasters

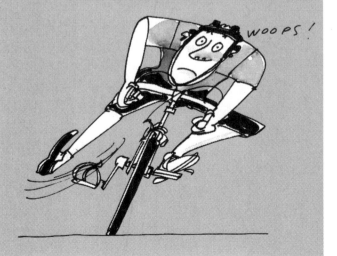
WOOPS!

A Hard Road

Cathy Watt was an Olympic hero in 1992 when she won the women's individual road race. The girl from country Victoria had started in track and field and won the National Junior 3000 metres before an Achilles tendon injury stopped her progress. She turned to cycling for rehabilitation and finished second in the National Individual Pursuit Title within a year. As further evidence of her ability she took part in the 1989 Australian Biathlon Championship involving cross-country skiing and shooting and finished third in 1989. She also competed in the 1991 World Mountain Bike Titles despite not having ridden one before the event. Watt's victory in Barcelona stamped her as a great champion but her build-up for Atlanta went wrong when she accused national track coach Charlie Walsh of instructing two riders to help opponents, rather than her, in a time trial. The 1996 Olympics saw the feud between Watt and Walsh reach a climax when rival rider Lucy Tyler-Sharman was selected ahead of her for the individual road race. Watt took action in the International Court for Arbitration in Sport, and won her case, but only a day before the event. Suffering nausea before the race she eventually finished ninth in the 58-woman field.

★★

Bad Blood

Relations between English and Australian cricketers reached a low level as early as 1879 when a bad umpiring decision by umpire George Coulthard resulted in William Murdoch being judged run out. The crowd was discontented by this dismissal and the Australian captain, David Gregory, refused to send another man in. The England captain Lord Harris went towards the pavilion to plead for the match to continue, but at this stage hundreds of spectators jumped the fence at the Sydney Ground and attacked both Lord Harris and other English cricketers. Lord Harris is reported to have been struck with a whip and Umpire Coulthard was also attacked. One English cricketer, Albert Hornby, took a blow but arrested his assailant and delivered him to police. It turned out that the trouble had been created by larrikins in the crowd, incited by some betting on the outcome. The *Sydney Morning Herald* described the events on the ground as a national humiliation and the New South Wales Cricket Association deputation apologised to Lord Harris over the riot. He accepted the apology, but said the events would not be easily forgotten.

Bad Decision

Champion footballer Greg 'Diesel' Williams was rejected by the club of his choice – Carlton – at the start of his career. He went to Geelong and then to Sydney before being lured to Carlton after having played for eight years and became the engine of the Carlton team. Williams won the Brownlow Medal while he was with the Sydney Swans in 1986.

Bad Show

Australia did so badly at the 1976 Olympics at Montreal, failing to score even one gold medal, that Prime Minister Malcolm Fraser instituted an inquiry into our sporting failure. The ultimate result was the establishment of the Australian Institute of Sport.

Beaten to Extinction

Victoria's University team dropped out of the Victorian Football League at the end of the 1914 season, having lost their last 51 matches. Some former University players crossed to Melbourne and improved the Melbourne team to the point that it had its best season in 13 years.

Boardroom Blows

It was a sensation at the Australian Cricket Board of Control meeting in 1912 when board member Peter McAllister told Australian Clem Hill that he was one of the worst captains that he had seen. Hill leant across the table and struck McAllister a blow on the face and they fought all around the office for about 20 minutes.

Bodyline

The idea of league theory or bodyline bowling was cooked up by England captain Douglas Jardine for the 1932/33 England Tour of Australia. Jardine had thought that Donald Bradman was suspect against a short rising ball aimed at the body and devised an attack lead by fast bowler Harold Larwood which would have batsmen fending off bouncers to a packed leg-side field. The ruse was partly effective as Bradman did battle against the bodyline attack, but he still managed to average 44 for the series. Stan McCabe did even better, defying the Englishman to hurt him and scoring magnificently, including 187 in the second Test in Sydney. The third Test in Adelaide brought matters to a head, and relations between Australia and England to crisis point. In Larwood's last ball off his second over to Australian Captain Bill Woodfull, the ball struck the captain above the heart. He staggered and dropped his bat. Soon afterwards the Australian wicketkeeper, Bert Oldfield, got hit on the head and suffered a hairline fracture of the skull. The crowd at Adelaide was incensed by the England attack and it seemed that a riot might break out, but nobody jumped the fence. Later Woodfall said to the England manager, Pelham Warner: 'There are two teams out there on the oval. One is playing cricket, the other is not. The game is too good to be spoiled.' In response to Woodfall's complaint, the Australian Board of Control telegrammed the MCC in London on 18 January saying that bodyline bowling was detrimental to the interests of the game and that 'in our opinion it is unsportsmanlike'. A series of cables then ensued between the Australian Board of Control and the MCC, and a compromise was reached in which Australia refrained from describing England's action as unsportsmanlike, but suggested that the particular class of bowling was not in the best interests of cricket. The remaining Tests were allowed to proceed. The cable war continued in discussions about the forthcoming England tour by Australia in 1934. Eventually the MCC cabled: 'Your team can certainly take the field with the knowledge and the full assurance that cricket will be played here in the same spirit as in the past.'

★★

Busby's Babes

Sir Matt Busby was a Scottish international who took over Manchester City in 1945 and engineered an FA Cup win in 1948. His 'Busby Babes' were a feared side in both English and European Soccer, but he died in the Munich air disaster in which Busby himself was seriously injured. As Sir Matt Busby, he later became Chairman of the English Football Association.

Chucked Out

In one of the great sagas of Australian cricket, fast bowler Ian Meckiff was no-balled by square leg umpire Col Egar four times in an over. The no-balls came in the second over (Meckiff's first) of South Africa's innings in the first Test in Brisbane in 1963. There had been speculation about Meckiff's bowling action but no one expected such a spectacular outcome, virtually excluding him from the game and a future first class career. Egar had watched Meckiff bowl some 119 overs in the Test and Shield matches before this game and he had in mind a directive from the Australian Board of Control that all umpires were to call any bowler whose action even hinted at any legality. Meckiff seems to have been a natural scapegoat as he had been called twice in the previous season and his action during England's 1958/59 tour of Australia caused concern and comment, mostly by English cricket writers. Lindsay Hasset, former Australian Cricket Captain wrote in *The Age* that he thought Meckiff's action could be doubted only rarely, and only became suspect when he was tired and lost balance at the moment of delivery. 'I have no doubt that Egar's action was honestly, even if wrongly, conceived. I would defy anyone to detect any difference in the deliveries,' Hassett said.

Clicked Out

Bertil Sandstrom of Sweden was placed second in the equestrian dressage at the 1932 Olympics but was relegated to last for encouraging his horse by making clicking noises. Sandstrom claimed that the noises were made by a creaking saddle.

Cricket Split

With many Australian senior players joining colleagues from around the world in Kerry Packer's rebel cricket organisation, Australia was left in a quandary regarding the Indian tour of 1977/78. The Board brought Bob Simpson out of retirement at the age of 41 to lead a piecemeal Australian team which included Jeff Thomson as vice-captain and debutants like Graeme Yallop, Craig Sergeant, Peter Toohey, David Ogilvie, Wayne Clark, Paul Hibbert and a new wicketkeeper, Steve Rixon. Despite the inexperience of the team, Australia won the series 3-2 in an absorbing contest. Meanwhile Packer's World Series cricket, boasting great names like Ian Chappell, Tony Greig, Dennis Lillee, Greg Chappell, David Hookes, Viv Richards, Andy Roberts and Gordon Greenidge attracted few spectators to their 'off broadway' venues. They came back to Australia in 1978/79 with a WSC Super Test Series, but again the crowds were unable to summon up any real interest. Meanwhile the official Australian team under the captaincy of Graham Yallop won a thrilling tussle with England but lost in the Ashes. The cricket war was declared over in May 1979, with Channel 9 securing telecast rights to Test cricket.

★★

Desperate Lunge

The 1991 World Cup Rugby Union win for the Australian Wallabies caused great excitement in the 'rugby states' of New South Wales and Queensland, and converted many devotees of the southern code of Australian Rules Football to more than a passing interest in the union game. On television they watched the Australian team, led by Nick Farr-Jones, receive their world cup medallions, and Farr-Jones and winger David Campese lift the cup in triumph. Towards the end of the match they had witnessed a rugby 'miracle' and English five-eighth Rob Andrew received a pass with the line 25 metres away. A try would have levelled the score, and Andrew set sail for the line, but Australian second-rower John Eales, 205 cm tall and not noted for his speed, somehow ran down and brought down the fastest man in the England team. Two minutes later the World Cup was in Australian hands. John Eales, who was to become known as the best of Australian Rugby Union players, had taken another step to greatness.

Desperate Swim

John Devitt's victory in the 100 metre freestyle final of the Rome Olympics at 1960 was controversial. Devitt and American Lance Larson swam desperately stroke for stroke to the line and finished in a flurry of water in what looked like a dead heat. Devitt looked across and saw Larson touch and was convinced that he had won, but an American friend of Larson walked over and told him he had won. He reacted by throwing his arms in the air and the crowd assumed that he had won. For 10 minutes they waited for the judges' decision and finally the announcement came: Devitt, Australia. The American team protested and the judges met to discuss their verdict. Two of the judges had called Devitt and one Larson but a second place judge had also voted for Devitt as the winner. So three thought Devitt had won and three thought Larson had won. The stopwatches which were used at the time showed Larson registering 55.1 seconds and Devitt 55.2. Despite this the chief judge ordered Larson's time changed to 55.2 and gave the decision to Devitt.

Drama of Mary Decker

American distance runner Mary Decker held 11 American records at eight different distances ranging from 800 to 10,000 metres. At the age of 13 she ran a mile in 4:55 and her career as a distance runner went to great heights. However

from 1974 onwards she suffered a series of injuries
– to her ankles, stress fractures in her lower legs,
and shin splints. Eventually her calf muscles grew
too large for their sheaths and she required an
operation. Tendonitis set in in 1979 but she came
back in 1980, setting a world record for the mile at
4:21.7 and an Olympic trial record at 4:04.91 for
the 1500 metres. Having missed the 1976 Olympics
because of her physical problems and the 1980
Games because of the US boycott of Moscow,
Decker set her hopes on 1984. She qualified for
the 1500 and 3000 metres, but decided to
concentrate on the 3000 metres, taking on the South
African-born Zola Budd, who was running for Great
Britain. Budd, who ran in bare feet, was a prodigy,
but untried in such a strong competition. Decker
led early in the race but Zola Budd passed her at
the 1600 metre mark. About 1000 metres later,
Decker, trying to surge to the lead, hit Budd's left
leg. This threw her off stride and she tripped over
and fell into the infield suffering a hip injury. Her
devastation over this occurrence led her to bitter
comments about Budd, but the South African was
exonerated from anywrongdoing.

★★

Dropping the Baton

One of the sensations of Australian athletics was the dropping-the-baton incident that occurred in the women's 4 x 100 metre relay at the 1952 Helsinki Olympic Games. It seemed certain that the Australian four of Marjorie Jackson, Shirley Strickland, Winsome Cripps and Verna Johnston would win gold for Australia as they had won their heat easily, breaking the world record. They were well in the clear as Cripps passed to Jackson at the last change-over, but the baton suddenly flew into the air and bounced on the track. It was caught on the rebound by Jackson but she was left behind the field. It transpired that Cripps had made a clean baton change over to Jackson and she was striding away when Cripp's knee collided with her arm, knocking the baton from her grasp. The incident robbed Jackson 'The Lithgow Flash', of three gold medals as she had broken world records in the 100 and 200 metres.

Drugs Cheat

Ben Johnson of Canada set a world record in the 100 metre sprint at Seoul, South Korea, but tested positive for steroids. Although he was not the first athlete to be disqualified, the high profile scandal rocked the sporting world.

★★

Dubious Honours

The dictatorial and underhand regime of the East Germans at the 1980 Moscow Olympics paid off when the women swimmers won 11 of 13 events and every one of the 54 rowers went home with a medal. Drugs and intense training created this unreal team of so-called super athletes.

★★

Falling Out

Fred Laver and Peter McAlister were great friends in their early days at the East Melbourne Cricket Club and shared in an amazing partnership exceeding 500 runs in a match against Fitzroy. They fell out, however, on a tour of England in which Laver was the manager and McAlister was the treasurer. McAlister did not keep any books because he said Laver had refused him information. Laver said he kept the books, but only as 'personal mementos'. Their enmity grew to bitter struggles at the Australian Cricket Board level.

First Drugs

The 1968 Olympics at Mexico City saw the first drug disqualification as a Swedish entrant in the modern pentathlon, Hans-Gunnar Liljenwall, tested positive for excessive alcohol.

Fisticuffs

The Australian tour of England in 1893 was such an unhappy affair that a train trip taking the team to Sussex ended in a violent fistfight – leaving the train compartment splattered with the players' blood. The tension and factional brawling was a result of lack of control by the team manager Victor Cohen and Captain Jack Blackham. The Australians' performance on the tour was so bad that they were attacked by the press with the *Bulletin* magazine maintaining the team's problem was they were unable to find an effective hangover cure after each night's celebration. The misery of the tour was compounded on the way home when they stopped over in America and lost to Philadelphia by a marginal 1 innings and 68 runs.

★★

Flying Visit

After a year off because of a knee injury, Hawthorn champion Peter Hudson returned in dramatic fashion with a helicopter landing him in VFL Park just before the start of play against Collingwood in 1973. Hudson kicked eight goals, but Hawthorn lost and Hudson flew back to Tasmania.

For Whom the Bell Tolls

In 1928 St Kilda won a match against Melbourne even though the winning goal was kicked at least seven seconds after the bell was sounded. The umpire didn't hear the bell despite its continual ringing. The tribunal verdict was that the score would stand.

Grand Final Thriller

In what is considered the greatest Grand Final of modern times, Hawthorn's Dermott Brereton was knocked out at the opening bounce but stayed on to become a star player. Geelong's Garry Ablett played the game of his life to kick nine goals and be named best on the ground. Hawthorn won by six points, 21.18 to 21.12.

Just One Slip

In one of those unforgettable sporting disasters, Shane Kelly from Ararat, Victoria, had a gold medal staring at him when he prepared for the one kilometre cycling time trial at Atlanta in 1996. He had won silver at Barcelona and was dubbed 'the minute man' after breaking 1.01 at the 1995 World Championships. He sat on his bike as his backers awaited the inevitable result, but as soon as he applied pressure to his pedal his foot slipped from his pedal strap and he was out of the race. He then did not bother to compete in the three lap race against the clock but rode a miserable lap, with his whole world in tatters. He vowed to overcome the experience by winning gold at Sydney, but his peak moment had passed and he was only able to take the bronze medal.

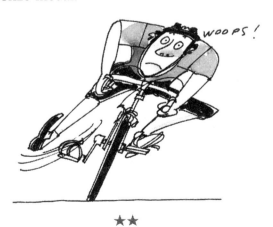

★★

Kidnapped

In an early scandal of cricket, the great English captain and batsman W.G. Grace kidnapped the young Australian all-rounder Billy Midwinter during the 1878 tour and took him off to play for Gloucestershire against Surrey. Midwinter was born in Gloucestershire but brought up on the Bendigo gold-fields, where his cricketing prowess saw his selection for the first Test match in 1877. Grace recognised his English beginnings and was determined to have him in his team.

Led by Lazarus

Melbourne Storm made an amazing beginning in the revamped National Rugby League competition in 1997. With very little hometown support, an indifferent media and a training ground in a park, the Storm carried all before them to get to the Preliminary Final. The Storm players were a 'foreign legion'. The most important signing was Glenn Lazarus, an Australian Test player who had the presence and big match experience to steady the developing side in their big matches.

★★

Left Behind

In a tremendous selection muddle, Sydney wicketkeeper Syd Deane was dropped from the Australian touring party after travelling from Sydney to Melbourne in the expectation that he would be among the 1890 Australians to go to England. He was replaced at the last minute by Tasmanian Kenny Burn, as the selector Harry Boyle had been told that Burn was a fine wicketkeeper. Burn however had never kept wickets in his life and the keeper in Tasmania who carried the same name had never received a message that he might be required for the tour. Burn joined the touring party and it was not until the ship was underway that Boyle's mistake was discovered.

Long Arm of the Law

A punch-up between Essendon and Richmond players and officials at Windy Hill at 1974 ended in mass suspensions, but also went to State Cabinet before a decision to charge Richmond President Graeme Richmond and player Steve Parsons was announced. They were cleared of police charges and, on the eve of the Grand Final, a Supreme Court Writ by Richmond prevented the implementation of fines imposed by the VFL.

★★

Marathon Disgrace

The marathon race at the 1904 St Louis Olympics was run in intense heat on dusty roads with clouds of dust being sent up by the cars of the officials and journalists who drove in front of the runners. The first person to finish was Fred Lorz of New York and he was about to be awarded the gold medal when it was discovered that he had stopped running after nine miles, ridden 11 miles in a car and then started running again. The winner was fellow American Thomas Hicks, who survived the difficult conditions by drinking a mixture of strychnine and brandy.

★★

Mass Tribute

When John Coleman, the greatest full forward of his time, died of a heart attack at his hotel in Dromana at the age of 44, the football world was shocked. A huge crowd gathered at St Thomas's Church in Moonee Ponds to pay tribute to Coleman on the day of his funeral.

Moscow Boycott

The Soviet invasion of Afghanistan in December 1979 caused the boycott of the Moscow Olympics by the United States and 64 other nations. Only 80 nations participated, the lowest number since 1956. The Australian Government supported the boycott but left the actual decisions on whether to attend to the various sporting organisations. The result was representation in some sports, non-attendance in others.

Political Football

The South African Rugby Union tour of 1971 is remembered more for the drama off the field than the play, as the tour attracted massive protests from those in opposition to South Africa's apartheid policies. The demonstrations included on-field invasions, the throwing of firecrackers and flour bombs onto playing arenas. A strong police presence was needed at all venues. The tour culminated in the declaration by Queensland Premier Joe Bjelke Petersen of a state of emergency to prevent further public disruption. Regardless of the pressure, the South African team showed its greatness playing 13 matches including three Tests and remaining undefeated, even though it had had little international competition due to its isolation in previous years.

★★

Racial Taunts

The Australian Football League introduced a Players' Code of Conduct in 1995 after Michael Long of Essendon was racially abused by Collingwood ruckman Damian Monkhorst. It has been invoked many times since, with Irishman ruckman Jim Stynes of Melbourne claiming to have been racially vilified.

★★

Rampaging Jonah Lomu

Perhaps the best known of all Rugby Union players is the huge New Zealand winger Jonah Lomu. The young man, who comes from a tough background in South Auckland, became the youngest All Black Test player, against France in 1994 at 19 years and 45 days. He hit centre stage in 1995 when he ran around and through his English opponents in a World Cup semi-final to score four tries. His size, his power, his speed and his on-field charisma made him the target for endorsements and he was soon the All Black with the highest earnings, despite his youth. A debilitating liver disease affected his career soon afterwards, but he is now back in the All Black line up, as daunting as ever.

Rueful Rueben

The Brisbane Bears owner Rueben Pelerman, who took over the AFL club in 1991, estimated he lost $3.3 million before giving away his private ownership. The Queensland businessman bought the team in a deal worth $10 million over five years and said it was an anniversary present for his wife.

Sacking Sensations

Melbourne's master coach of the '50s and '60s, Norm Smith, was sensationally sacked in 1965 after being critical of the committee. Smith was reinstated after four days when players and staff threatened to resign and former player Ron Barassi's anger had reduced the club secretary, Jim Cardwell, to tears. There have been many similar sackings: the crude removal of Footscray's favourite son Charlie Sutton in favour of a new hero Ted Whitten, and the sudden St Kilda decision to dispense with coaching icon Malcolm Blight in the first season with the club. Only two seasons before that Stan Alves was shown the door at St Kilda, only a year since he had brought the team to a Grand Final. Richmond has not been the same since it decided to dispense with Tom Hafey, while John Northey had built a team at Melbourne before he saw the writing on the wall. The cruelty and the irony of sackings goes on and on.

Sad End (1)

It was a dramatic and sad moment for Australian cricket when Captain Kim Hughes resigned in 1984, shortly after the loss to the West Indies in the first Test in Brisbane. Hughes's style of captaincy and a series of poor results had brought heaps of criticism upon him in the press and by former players. Allan Border was elevated to the captaincy.

Sad End (2)

Although only 28 when he retired Reg Gasnier had a century of Test tries to his credit and had played a then record 36 Tests for Australia. Gasnier was forced out by injury. He was captain coach on the 1967 Kangaroo tour, but sustained a broken leg in the first Test loss. Australia retained the Ashes, but Gasnier tried to make a premature return in a provincial match in France, and was forced from the field. He then announced his retirement. Gasnier was a rugby genius, a brilliant runner and try scorer, but also a team player with a sportsmanlike manner. After showing out at his club St George he burst on to the wider stage with three tries on debut for St George and a further three in the second Test against New Zealand.

Saints on Strike

With all but seven of its players on strike in 1911, boys were rounded from the street to make up a team to play Essendon. They were thrashed 23.10 to 5.8. The strike arose when the committee withdrew passes for the players' family and friends to attend the game.

★★

Short-term Coach

When Collingwood appointed Bervyn Woods as coach for the 1950 season after Jock McHale's retirement, the decision was greeted with anger and incredulity. The favourite for the job, Phonse Kyne, received a £200 cheque from wealthy supporter John Wren with a note that the decision was 'amazing and incomprehensible'. Woods resigned after he was jeered at at Collingwood's final practice match and Kyne was installed in the job. There were further repercussions when the old guard of the committee, President Harry Curtis, Frank Wraith and Bob Rush – who had voted for Woods – were outed by members at a mass meeting at the Collingwood Town Hall.

Smart Start

Brad Fittler was the first player to graduate straight from an Australian schoolboys' side to a senior Australian Rugby League team when he made his Test debut against Papua New Guinea in 1991. In 1990 he became the youngest player in State of Origin history at 18 years and 114 days, and then toured with the Kangaroos. He had played in six matches for NSW, four tests, 13 tour games and a World Cup Final before his 21st birthday.

★★

Smashing Time

In 1918 when the Victorian Football League decided to put beer at the ground at sixpence per glass, the public responded by wrecking a beer booth at the semi-final between Collingwood and St Kilda, smashing every glass on the premises.

★★

Snow Job

Perhaps it was the length of the series that drove the England team to an incident-packed departure from the field in the seventh Test against Australia. The Test in Sydney saw trouble brewing early when the crowd on the hill erupted into a brawl 15 minutes before tea. The trouble began when Terry Jenner, the Australian tail-ender, was hit by a bouncer from John Snow. Umpire Rowe warned Snow for intimidatory bowling and Snow snatched his cap and stalked away to his fielding position under the hill. Snow walked right to the fence and swapped comments with jeering spectators. One drunken barracker grabbed Snow by the shirt as the cans flew in the bowler's direction. England captain Ray Illingworth signalled to the rest of the team to follow him off the ground without a word to either the umpires or the batsmen. Within minutes Illingworth's team came back after having been told by the umpires that the game could be given to Australia if they did not return. The bad-tempered series ended with victory to England, with two wins and four drawn games.

Solomon's Cap

Among the many excitements of the 1961 tour of Australia by the West Indies was the incident of Joe Solomon's cap. In the Melbourne second Test, Australia won by seven wickets after a subdued batting performance by the West Indies. The West Indies' second innings was set back when opener Joe Solomon could not get his head out of the way of a delivery by spin bowler and captain Richie Benaud and his cap fell off and dislodged a bail. Benaud and wicketkeeper Wally Grout appealed and Solomon was given out, much to the displeasure of the crowd and later condemnation by some cricketing journalists. Later in the innings, a Benaud delivery hit the wicket when Gerry Alexander was on 25, but this time the bail did not come off. Later in that series, the outcome of the fourth Test in Adelaide came down to a last wicket partnership between Australians Ken 'Slasher' Mackay and Lindsay Kline. Kline was a noted rabbit batsman. However he hung on with Mackay to force a draw in the match. In the final overs, Kline was surrounded by all 10 fieldsmen, none more than metres from the bat. The exciting series was finally won by Australia in the fifth Test at the Melbourne Cricket Ground when Australia won by two wickets.

★★

Sound of Rugby

The voice of Australian Rugby League for many decades was Rex 'The Moose' Mossop, sometimes known for the near incoherence of his calls when the game got exciting. Mossop started in Rugby Union with the Manly Club, and played in five Tests for Australia before turning professional to play in England. On his return, he joined the Manly Sea Eagles in Rugby League.

Star Material

With the look of excellence written all over him Michael Cleary was a champion at three sports, and later became Minister for Sport. The superbly built Cleary joined Randwick Rugby Union Club and was capped for Australia in his second season, 1961. The following year he joined South Sydney Rugby League club, but kept his amateur status and competed in the Commonwealth Games at Perth, winning a bronze medal in the 100 metres. In 1964 he won a match race with the other 'fastest man in the league' Ken Irvine. Cleary showed that speed again when he scored a length of the field try in South's 1968 Grand Final win over Manly. He played in five Kangaroo tours.

Strike Averted

Richmond players in the VFL threatened to strike in 1944 after centre man Jack Broadstock was suspended for eight weeks 'for having kicked or intended to kick' an opponent. The strike was only averted when the president, Mr H. Dyke, told him that he would field the second's team rather than forfeit the game. The Tigers won, but lost in the Grand Final a week later.

★★

Super Boot

All Black Don Clarke is the greatest distance kicker in Rugby Union, and he became known to fans and opposing teams alike as 'The Boot' when he played from 1956 to 1964. His greatest match was in the second Test of the 1960 New Zealand tour of South Africa. With South Africa 11-3 ahead and five minutes remaining he kicked a booming penalty goal from just short of his own 10 metre line. A few minutes later he converted a try to level the scores.

Terrifying Win

Ralph Doubell collapsed after winning the 800 metre gold medal at the 1968 Mexico City Olympics. The extreme effort in the thin air of Mexico's elevated capital left Doubell dangerously depleted in oxygen. The favourite for the medal was Kenya's Wilson Kiprugut, a runner well used to high altitude athletics. Doubell's race plan, devised by his coach Franz Stampfl, was for him to stay back in the field and let Kiprugut set the pace in front. Doubell settled in fifth or sixth position where he watched Kiprugut set up a five-metre lead. Then Doubell took off. He said later: 'I came up to him with 80 metres to go, and for the first 30 he was still with me. I thought I had him about there, though for those first 30 metres up the straight I wasn't so sure. As I finally passed him I was screaming to myself: 'Christ, I can win it. I can win!' Doubell's time of 1:44.3 equalled the world record of Peter Snell of New Zealand.

The Old Mug

The America's Cup, the most prized trophy in yachting, originated as the Hundred Guinea Cup, put up by the Royal Yacht Club of Britain, for a 58 mile race around the Isle of Wight. The British had invited the Americas to be part of a regatta which coincided with the World Fair in 1851. The New York Yacht club put up a specially designed yacht *America*. The NYYC Commodore John Stevens offered a match race with any British yacht, but the British, seeing the raked masts and the cotton sails which looked trimmer than the flax sails commonly in use, declined. *America* then raced in the Isle of Wight race and won by 18 minutes. The six-man syndicate that owned *America* gave the cup to the NYYC, with a deed of gift specifying that it was to be offered as a trophy to be challenged for by any foreign yacht club. The race has attracted intense rivalry and has often been marred by controversy. After two apparent wins by England were upset by NYYC rulings a British writer commented in 1934: 'Britannia rules the waves, but America waives the rules.' When Australia's *Gretel II* was disqualified after winning a race in 1967, there were howls of protest, even from Americans who thought the NYYC was being unfair. In the Australian parliament there were calls for the Australian Ambassador to the US to be withdrawn. After holding the Cup for 132 years and 25 challenges the USA surrendered it in 1983 to the challenger *Australia II*, owned by the since disgraced businessman Alan Bond. This was the smallest yacht ever to compete for the race, but its secret was a keel fitted with 'wings', which made it very fast and manoeuvrable. The NYYC tried to have the yacht given a different rating so that it would be ineligible to challenge, but the International Yacht Racing Union refused to intervene. After being behind three races to one in the seven-race series, *Australia II*, skippered by John Bertrand, won the final three races and the cup.

★★

Tragic Error

Irish footballer Jim Stynes made the mistake of his life when he ran across the mark of Hawthorn player Garry Buckenara after Buckenara was free kicked in the dying moments of a preliminary final. The mistake gave Buckenara a 15-metre penalty and he was then close enough to score a winning goal. The Irishman Stynes was unaware that he had broken a rule in his adopted game. Just seven years after he first kicked an Australian football, 25-year-old Irishman Jim Stynes won the Brownlow Medal in 1991. The Melbourne ruckman had answered a Melbourne Football Club advertisement in Ireland for recruits to Australian Rules football. The Demons also picked up a brilliant player in Sean White.

Unlucky Raelene

Raelene Boyle was unlucky in her quest for an Olympic gold medal and had her hopes dashed when she was disqualified from the 200 metre semi-finals at the 1976 Montreal Olympics. Raelene was a hot favourite to win the race as she had been in five Olympic sprint finals, winning three silver medals and seemed the best-qualified runner in the field. In her semi-final however, an electronic starting device registered a clean start but the recall judge stopped the race, later claiming that Raelene had rolled her head and shoulders forward while waiting on the blocks for the start. Unaware that she had been credited with a false start (she did not receive the customary warning) Raelene false-started again and was therefore automatically disqualified. She had no reason for breaking the second time but there was no chance to redo the damage and Raelene was out of the event. Raelene Boyle has lent her personality and prestige in recent years to publicising efforts to prevent breast cancer. She has suffered two bouts of cancer herself, but has overcome the disease. She was recently honoured in a black tie evening in Melbourne to celebrate her fiftieth birthday.

Wrong Place

Fitzroy policeman and defender Bill Marchbank was refused leave from the police force to play against Richmond in 1910. He went to the football instead as a mounted policeman on duty, and broke his leg on a post while working at the South Melbourne and Essendon game.

Chapter 3

Heroes of the Sporting World

All Ten

Western Australian swing bowler Ian Brayshaw had the match of his life in 1967 when he took all Victorian first innings wickets at a match in Perth. Brayshaw finished with 10/44 off 17.6 overs. The only other man to take all 10 wickets in a Sheffield Shield innings were Tim Wall of New South Wales and Peter Allan of Victoria.

All the Records

At one stage in her career, Shane Gould held every world freestyle record from 100 metres to 1500 metres. She achieved her greatest triumphs at the 1972 Munich Olympics when she won three gold medals in the 200 metre freestyle, 400 metre freestyle and 200 metre individually medley, a silver medal in the 800 metre freestyle and a bronze medal in the 100 metre freestyle. She was named Australian of the Year in that year of 1972. By the end of 1973 she retired and disappeared from public life, particularly after her marriage and move to Western Australia.

An Inspiration

South Sydney Rugby League captain John Sattler inspired his team to victory in the 1970 Rugby League Grand Final. After only 10 minutes of play Sattler was felled by a punch from a Manly-Warringah forward and suffered a double fracture of the jaw. He said to his winger Mike Cleary, 'Help me up, so they don't know I'm hurt', and continued to play in the torrid game. Sattler's other team mate learned of his injury at half time, but he refused attention and returned to the field to lead his team to a decisive 23-12 victory. Only after receiving the Giltinan Shield did he go to hospital.

Atlanta Hero

Kieren Perkins's heroic win in the 1500 metres at Atlanta electrified Australia but he performed even better in the 1992 Barcelona Olympics when he went through the 800 metres of the 1500 metre event in 7:48:27, the third fastest time in history. Perkins turned it on to finish in 14:43:48. He had swum 4.90 seconds under his own world record.

Barassi's Dad

Ron Barassi's father, Ron Barassi Snr, played on the wing for Melbourne before joining the army during World War II and losing his life in the siege of Tobruk in 1941. The 'Last Post' was played in his memory before the Melbourne Collingwood game on 16 August 1941. Ron Barassi started his illustrious career in 1953.

Brave Bev

Beverley Buckingham won the 1981-1982 Tasmanian Jockey's Premiership with 63 wins. She was the first woman in any Australian state to top the Jockey's list. She began riding races at the age of 15, apprenticed to her trainer father. After riding 1000 winners, Buckingham was hurt in a four-horse fall at Elwick in 1998. She was catapulted into the air and landed on her back. She vowed to overcome her terrible injuries but her racing career was finished. As Beverley Buckingham-Smith she was named the 1998 personality of the year by the Victorian Racing Club and the Victorian Racing Media Association. She has carried on her career with horses as a trainer.

Canny Campo

David Campesi was noted for his elusive running as a fullback or winger for the Australian Wallabies. He became the leading try scorer in International Rugby Union with 64 tries to his credit, and Australia's most capped Test player with 101 Tests. He was unanimously hailed as the best player of the 1991 World Cup, won by Australia. He had a trademark 'goose step' which had opponents groping at air as he bamboozled them by changing course.

Cathy Comes Through

Never before has an Australian athlete carried such hopes, and such pressure, as Cathy Freeman as she lined up for the final of the Olympic 400 metres. Her rivalry with the absent French star Marie-Jose Perec (who left the Games early), her flag-carrying for her Aboriginal people, her selection to light the Olympic flame, the questions of Aboriginal reconciliation on the political agenda – all this rested on those slim shoulders – shrouded this time in a green all-in-one running suit. She started well, but not brilliantly. She stayed with the field, but did not streak away. She reached the final bend on terms with her opponents and then, with one surge of power, she was clear and powering for the line – for glory and relief.

★★

Clarence Comet

Henry Searle was a talented sculler and defeated fellow Australian Peter Kemp to win the Australian title in 1888. Lacking Australian challengers, Searle went to London where he easily defeated the American professional champion. During the trip home he contracted typhoid and died in Melbourne in 1889. The outpouring of public grief in response to his death indicates the extreme popularity of the sport of sculling in nineteenth-century Australia. A column to the memory of Henry Searle, also known as the 'Clarence Comet', stands at the finishing line of the Old Parramatta River Sculling Course.

Coleman's Leap

Essendon's John Coleman, who was considered to be one of the finest of full forwards, had a prodigious leap. In one match in 1950 North Melbourne back pocket Pat Kelly said that he looked up for the ball and was flabbergasted to see the soles of John Coleman's boots. 'He had jumped clean over my head,' said Kelly.

★★

Constable Coach

Allan 'Yabbie' Geans, one of the most successful coaches of modern times with St Kilda and Hawthorn, was a policeman over his nearly 40-year career, finishing as a Senior Sergeant. His coaching style emphasised discipline and self-discipline. He once said that football was like cooking sausages – you could fry them, curry them, put applesauce with them, but they were still sausages. The basics are still the basics.

Courageous Clive Churchill

The quality of South Sydney's fullback Clive Churchill was demonstrated in the Rugby League club's 1955 Premiership season. South Sydney lost the first match of the second round and they were virtually playing to stay in the competition in the race for the finals. A big test came early in the match against Manly when Churchill broke his forearm. There were no replacements in those days and Churchill refused to come off the field. He had a painkilling injection and his left arm encased in a cardboard cast. Churchill continued to tackle as hard as ever and his play was such an inspiration to his team mates that, five minutes from the end of the match, winger Ian Moir scored a try to level the score. Captain-coach Jack Reynard threw the ball to Churchill to complete the kick to determine whether or not South remained in the running for the Premiership. Despite his handicap, the fullback placed the ball and kicked it through the post for a great victory.

Dominator

When Michael Johnson took the blocks for the 1996 400 metres at the Atlanta Olympics, he had dominated the event to such an extent that he won 54 straight finals since April 1989. He won the 1993 and 1995 World Championships but, because of food poisoning in 1992, he had not won an Olympic gold medal in an individual event. Johnson cruised effortlessly through the opening rounds and the finals and after the semi-final he threw his shoes into the stands, forgetting that they had rather sharp spikes on them. He appeared for the final wearing gold shoes. Into the final he quickly opened a five-metre lead and continued to pull away until he crossed the finishing line 10 metres ahead. Johnson competed the dose in his final Olympic appearance at Sydney 2000.

Double Firsts

Arthur Morris, who became an outstanding Test opener for Australia, was the first player in the world to score a century in each innings of his debut first class match, for New South Wales against Queensland in 1940. His Test career was interrupted by war but he made 12 centuries in 46 Tests.

Double Triple

Jimmy Matthews playing for Australia in 1912 scored a unique double in his first Test. He took a double hat trick, one in each innings of the same match on the same day and remains the only bowler to have done so in first-class cricket. Matthews was a leg break bowler with a good mixture of deliveries and he bamboozled the South African batsman in the triangular series between England, Australia and South Africa, held in England. South African wicketkeeper Tom Ward was a hat trick victim in both innings. Strangely, Matthews did not take any other wickets in the match.

Duncan's Game

Carlton's centre halfback Alex Duncan took 33 marks in a game against Collingwood in 1927 in a display described as the best ever. His aerial work was perfection and his beautiful dropkicking completed a magnificent match. Only Ron Clegg from South Melbourne has come close to Duncan's performance, taking 32 marks in a match against Fitzroy in 1951.

Enduring Ron Clarke

Ron Clarke, who lit the Olympic flame at the 1956 Games in Melbourne, went on to break more official world records for running than any other athlete in history, but sadly he was never able to win an Olympic gold medal. Clarke broke a total of 18 world records, ranging from two miles upwards. His most spectacular record effort was in trimming 35.8 seconds off the world 10,000 metre record and his most spectacular run of records occurred in 1965, when he set 12 world records on a 44-day tour of Europe.

Fabulous Fammo

Jean Pierre 'Johnny' Famechon was the son and nephew of French professional boxers and began his own career at the age of 16. He won the World Title against Jose Legra of Spain and retained it against a Japanese opponent, Fighting Harada. In that fight he survived three knockdowns and the referee ruled the fight a draw, but Famechon won after Harada demanded a recount. The judge's tally had Famechon in front by a point. Famechon lost his title in 1970 and retired a few weeks later. He has bravely battled paralysis and mental difficulties after being knocked down by a motor vehicle in 1991.

Fearsome Duo

The greatest bowling pair to play for Australia were Dennis Lillee and Jeff Thomson, a fearsome duo of fast bowlers. Sharing the new ball, Lillee and Thomson played together in 25 Tests from 1974 to 1983, capturing 214 wickets. Lillee's contribution was 116 while Thomson's was 98. Lillee had a classical style, a long menacing run up, high bounding action and a copybook follow through. He bowled fast and mixed his pace with in swingers and out swingers, teasing and tempting the batsman. Thomson had been a champion javelin thrower and his bowling style was something of that action. He hurled missiles at the batsmen, intimidating them with rising balls that were a severe physical threat. They played in a time before batsmen wore helmets, and no doubt some of the English batsmen in the 1974/1975 tour of Australia were genuinely disturbed by the fear of injury.

First African

Abebe Bikila ran barefoot in the marathon at the Rome Olympics in 1960, to become the first black African Olympic champion. He won a marathon for Ethiopia, a country that had once been colonised by his host nation Italy. Bikila proved his greatness four years later by winning again.

First Superstar

The most decorated champion of the ancient Olympics was the runner Leonidas of Rome, who won 12 championships between 164 BC and 152 BC. The most famous of ancient athletes was the wrestler Milon of Kroton. After winning the wrestling contest in 540 BC, he won five times between 532 BC and 516 BC until he was finally defeated by Timasitheos of Croton.

★★

First Test Hero

When Australia won the first Test match against England in Melbourne, the hero was Charles Bannerman, an opening batsman who made 165 not out in the first innings. He helped Australia to a total of 245. This enabled a final victory by 45 runs which was, coincidentally, the same margin of victory by Australia in the Centenary Test played on the same cricket ground 100 years later. Charles Bannerman died in 1930, but in that year he was at the Sydney Cricket Ground to see young Don Bradman score 452 not out for New South Wales, then a record first class score. The two men were photographed together. The first Test was another spur towards the Federation of Australia. After the victory *The Argus* said the next day: 'For the time being, we all, New South Wales and Victorians must forget our geographical distinctions and only remember that we are of one nation, Australia. ' The players who won the first Test match received a gold medal from the Victorian Cricketers Association while £83 was raised for Charles Bannerman, and £23 each for bowler Tom Kendall and wicketkeeper Jack Blackham.

★★

Gabba's Run

Gay Gabelich, captain of Collingwood, nearly brought his team glory in the 1964 Grand Final when he made a gallant 60-yard dash for the goal line and scored. The 17 stone Collingwood skipper bounced the ball three times and nearly lost it each time, but finally got to the goal before the Melbourne defenders caught him. His efforts went for nothing when a few minutes later, Melbourne back pocket Neil Crompton casually took a ball off the pack and kicked a goal to get the four point winning margin.

Globetrotting Herb

Herb Gilbert was one of the pioneers of Australian Rugby League. A product of South's Rugby Union club, he played three Tests against the All Blacks in 1910, before joining South's Rugby League club. He was a member of the touring Kangaroos in England in 1911-12, and top scored in the Ashes win with 20 tries. So great was his prowess that he was lured to the English club Hull for the then record signing fee of 450 pounds, leading the club to victory in the 1914 final. On his return to Sydney he played with Souths, Easts and Wests in successive years, before seeing out his career with St George, becoming a coach and selector with the club. His sons Herb, Jack and Bob all played with St George.

★★

Golden Heroine

All of Australia took Betty Cuthbert to their hearts after she had won three gold medals at the 1956 Melbourne Olympics. The unassuming blonde 18-year-old won the 100 metres, 200 metres and was part of the winning 4 x 100 metre relay team. She ran with her mouth wide open, presumably to gulp in oxygen. Images of her victory were on the front pages of every newspaper and she was tagged as 'The Golden Girl'. Her Melbourne efforts continued when she represented Australia at the Rome Olympics, but she was suffering from injury and lost her titles to America's Wilma Rudolph. Four years later she won her fourth gold medal in the 400 metres at Tokyo. In recent years she has battled multiple sclerosis, but her occasional public appearances were highlighted by the opening day at the Sydney Olympics, as she was one of those who passed the Olympic Flame to Cathy Freeman.

Good Sport

British fencer Judy Guinness gave up her gold medal in 1932 when she pointed out to officials that they had not noticed two scores against her by her opponent Ellen Preis of Austria.

Goodiwindi Grey

Grey racehorse Gunsynd was idolised by the racing public as he won many races in New South Wales and Victoria. The grey colt was raised by a syndicate in Goondiwindi, Queensland, and became known as the Goondiwindi Grey. He set his career up by winning his first four races and then was transferred to trainer Tommy Smith in Sydney to become a premier racehorse of his time from 1970 to 1972.

Hero's Welcome

When squadron leader Keith 'Bluey' Truscott DFC and Bar returned to Melbourne in 1942 on leave, he was given the honour of playing and leading the Melbourne team out, even though he was not fit. Truscott was later killed in training off the coast of Western Australia, but he is remembered at the club with the Truscott Trophy for the best and fairest player.

Heroic Stand

Captain Allan Border and tail ender Jeff Thomson electrified Australia with their heroic last wicket stand in the fourth Test against England in Melbourne in 1982. When Thomson came to the crease, Australia needed 37 runs to win and England needed one wicket. The first nine overs of the morning produced 0, 2, 0, 1, 0, 1, 3, 1, 3. The pair declined to play 29 seemingly easy singles and the tension was almost unbearable when just four runs short of victory England's Ian Botham came into the attack. Thomson edged Botham's first ball to first slip where Chris Tavare fumbled, but keeper Geoff Miller dived to snatch the catch and withhold victory from Australia.

Hot Babe

American Babe Didrikson, aged 18, qualified for all five women's track and field events in 1932 in Los Angeles. She was only allowed to compete in three. She won the javelin throw and set world records in the high jump and the 80 metre hurdles. She later became a golf champion.

★★

Hustling Herb

Herb Elliott's victory in the 1500 metres at the Rome Olympics stamps him as one of the greatest athletes of the century. He had won over 44 consecutive races over a mile or 1500 metres before he lined up for that final and he won it by 18 metres in a world record of 3:35.6. Elliott's rush for victory came after his coach Percy Cerutty had waved a white towel at him to tell him that this was the time to step on the gas.

★★

I am the Greatest

The Muhammad Ali saga hit the headlines in 1960 when the young light-heavyweight Cassius Clay, a Black African from Louisville, Kentucky, won the Olympic gold medal. He later threw the medal into a river as a symbol of defiance against racist America, when he and a companion had been thrown out of a bar. Clay turned pro and started to make a name for himself and fought Sonny Liston for the heavyweight title in 1964, winning what had been seen to be a mismatch when Liston failed to come out for the seventh round. Cassius Clay, handsome and extroverted, became known as the 'Louisville Lip' for his bragging and pre-fight predictions. 'I'm young, I'm handsome, I'm smart and I just can't be beaten. I am the greatest' is definitely one of the top quotes in sporting folklore. As is: 'I float like a butterfly, and sting like a bee.' Clay shocked the boxing world, and became a symbol of black defiance, when he became a Black Muslim and changed his name to Muhammad Ali. He also refused induction for the Vietnam War, was sentenced to five years in prison for draft evasion, and was stripped of his boxing licence and titles. Ali appealed the sentence and his lawyers worked to get him a boxing licence. Finally, the city of Atlanta granted him a licence to fight the white hope, Jerry Quarry, in 1970. Ali won in three rounds, in a fight watched by more than half a million paying customers on closed circuit television. A New York judge ordered Ali's full licence restored and he went on to attempt to reclaim his crown from Joe Frazier in a fight described by the *New York Times* as 'an exhibition of primitive savagery'. Frazier staved off defeat when he knocked Ali down with a left hook in the fifteenth round. With his conviction set aside by the New York Supreme Court Ali started to scale the heights again, beating Frazier in a 12-rounder, and finally facing the new champion George Foreman, in a match staged in 1974 in Kinshasa, Zaire, the first heavyweight World Championship fight ever staged in Africa. The world's press turned out for this test of nerve in a bizarre setting, with the two boxer's camps playing mind games as the fight approached. In the ring Ali unveiled a new strategy, which he called 'Rope-a-Dope'. He would lean against the ropes with his arms shielding his torso and his gloves protecting his face. Foreman kept hitting at this defensive ball with little effect and tired himself to the point that Ali dispatched him in the eighth round. The whole episode can be seen in the award-winning documentary film *Once They Were Kings*. Ali defended the title three times before the next blockbuster *Thriller In Manila* when he faced Frazier in 1975. Ali completed the circle when he knocked out Frazier in the fourteenth round. The Vietnam War had divided the nation and at its end Ali was seen as a national hero, a symbol of defiance against both racism and American militarism. His last great fights were against Leon Spinks and he finally retained his title and retired undefeated in 1978. An ill-considered comeback attempt slightly diminished his stature, but on his retirement for good his record stood at 61 professional victories, 56 victories, 37 by KO. He was knocked out only once. He was affected in later life, however, by Parkinson's disease, which left him shaking and speechless, but with his famous fighting spirit intact. The enduring image of the 1996 Olympics is of Ali's shaking hand moving a taper to light the Olympic flame.

Jezza's Magic

In one of the finest passages of football, Alex Jesaulenko of Carlton kicked six goals in 11 minutes as his team piled on 12 goals for a quarter against Essendon. Jesaulenko also gave away another couple of goals to David McKay and Brent Crosswell.

Jock McHale's Record

The outstanding service of Jock McHale to the Collingwood Football club has made him the most influential figure in the club's history. McHale was all Collingwood. He played 261 games, coached for more than 700 and was part of 10 of the Club's Premierships including the famous four in a row from 1927 to 1930. In his playing days, from 1903 to 1917, he mostly played as a centre man and showed great cunning as well as skill, but it was his consistency that was most remarkable. He played 191 games in a row from 1906 to 1917. He started coaching in 1912 and the Magpies were finalists in 27 of the 38 years in which he coached. McHale was a quiet man by nature, but his passion for Collingwood was such that he delivered soul-stirring half-time addresses that could lift players to the heights. Although his players revered him he kept apart from them and many only referred to him as Mr McHale or 'Sir'. He retired just before the start of the 1950 season and died of a heart attack the day after the Magpies had won the 1953 Premiership.

★★

Last Post

A football match between St Kilda and Essendon stopped dead in 1922 as a bugler marched on the ground to play the 'Last Post'. He was commemorating the death of Lieutenant James Bennett, an aviator who died in England in a crash on the eve on an attempted round-the-world flight with Captain Ross Smith. St Kilda barracker Bennett was given a state funeral and the funeral procession was passing the St Kilda ground when the bugler appeared.

Last Straw

On the eve of going to War, Dr Roy Park was suspended for four weeks for striking an opponent while playing for Melbourne against St Kilda. Park had three witnesses to say he was nowhere near the player who was felled. He announced his retirement as he went to collect his military uniform.

Late Developer

Yachtsman Bill Northam won a gold medal in Tokyo in 1964 when he was a 59-year-old grandfather. The former motor racing driver and successful businessman took up sailing at the age of 46 and became expert in the 5.5 metre class. Northam and his crew sailed well and had an opportunity to win the gold medal as they went into the final race. For a period it looked like America would win, as Sweden and America went to the front with a freak puff of wind. Northam said later that his crew told him to just concentrate on sailing, but 'we're gone'. Northam looked up and saw that America was ahead, but to the leeward of Sweden. He realised that the American was too far to the leeward and the Swede would take him right into the flag at the leeward end of the line. Northam came about and went for the line, while America tacked and tried to clear Sweden's bow, but it had no hope and the boats collided. Northam's boat crossed the line second and won the gold medal on accumulated points.

Local Hero

The real hero of the 1896 Olympic Games held in Athens was Spiridon Louis, a 24-year old Greek shepherd who won the 40,000 metre marathon race. The race was created in the honour of Pheidippides who carried the news of a Greek victory at the Battle of Marathon and dropped dead on delivering his message. Louis won the race by more than seven minutes.

★★

Long Innings

John Rantall, who created a VFL record when he played his three hundred and thirty-fourth game in 1980 did it with three clubs. He played 260 games for South, 70 games for North and finally lined up with Fitzroy, always as a specialist halfback flanker.

Lost Hero

Les Darcy was a great name in early Australian boxing. The country youngster, who was a blacksmith by trade, was still only 20 when he had won 46 of 50 professional fights between 1910 and 1916. At the height of his powers he was the greatest middleweight fighter in the world. Darcy's career came to a tragic end. He was branded a shirker because he did not enlist in the AIF for World War I service. In an attempt to further his boxing career he stowed away in a ship to the United States, but was refused permission to fight there. He became ill from infected teeth and died in Memphis, Tennessee. His body was brought home and there was a huge and emotional funeral at his hometown of Maitland, New South Wales.

★★

Madame Butterfly

Susie O'Neill was a favourite with swimming fans for her brilliant efforts at the butterfly event and had earned the title Madame Butterfly. The highlight of her career was her victory in the women's 200 metre butterfly in 1996 Olympics when she beat Ireland's Michelle Smith who had won three gold medals before their race. O'Neill finished her career in stunning fashion at the Sydney Olympics. She won the 200 metre freestyle against a champion field, but had to be content with second in her favourite event, to American Misty Hyman. At the end of the Games Susie O'Neill was one of eight athletes inducted into the International Olympic Committee. She later retired, having won 33 Australian swim championship victories and a medal in every international.

★★

Massie's Match

In the greatest debut ever by a Test fast bowler, Western Australia's Bob Massey massacred the English in the second Test in 1972, which Australia won by eight wickets. Massey's figures were 8/84 and 8/53. The medium pacer had an uncanny ability to swing the ball and bowled perfectly as the English batsman fell to his changes of pace and swing in both directions. People rose to their feet as Massey walked back to the rooms and then a hush descended on Lords – 'Who was this man?' they whispered. Massie had a good season in England but in later seasons he was unable to control his prodigious swing and he dropped out of first-class cricket. He is now a respected commentator with the ABC.

Master Boxer

Cuban super heavyweight, Teofilo Stevenson became the first boxer to win the same weight division three times at the 1980 Moscow Olympics. Stevenson was regarded as the natural successor to the world professional heavyweight title but refused to change his amateur status. He said he fought only for his country and did not which to be sullied by the professional sport.

Master Coach

Rick Charlesworth has had an outstanding sporting career but not content with that he has also gained success in his chosen profession, medicine, and then as a Federal Labor politician. Charlesworth was a natural sportsman who played as an opening batsman for Western Australia, scoring more than 2000 runs. Off the field he completed a medical degree and in 1983 he became Federal Labor MP for Perth. His main sport, however, was hockey. He captained the Western Australia hockey team and was involved in winning 13 national titles out of the 17 his team contested. He competed in the Australian hockey team at four Olympic Games, from Munich in 1972 to Seoul 1988, winning a silver medal with the team at Montreal in 1976. The Australians were cruelly robbed of a medal at Montreal as they were hot favourites going into the final against a New Zealand team that had conceded more goals than they had scored. A penalty goal by Tony Ineson early in the second half gave New Zealand a 1 – 0 victory. Charlesworth has had great success as coach of the all-conquering women's team, the Hockeyroos, winning two Olympic and two Commonwealth gold medals, two World Titles and four champion trophies.

★★

Match Record

Michael Tuck began his football career at Hawthorn as an 18-year-old in 1972 and ended it as captain in 1991 with a record 426 games. He played in 13 Premierships and won the Order of Australia Medal.

Memories of Ted

Mr Football, E. J. 'Ted' Whitten, died in 1995, but the memories of a great player and great character linger on. There is an E. J. Whitten stand at his beloved Western Oval with a statue of Ted in the park outside, an E. J. Whitten bridge on the Western Ring Road in Melbourne, an E.J. Whitten Medal for the best player in State of Origin Football between South Australia and Victoria.

Mighty Mick

Michael Doohan is the darling of Australian motorcycle fans, having won 46 Grand Prix in the 500CC event, including 10 in a row. He made his Grand Prix debut in 1989 and won the World Title in 1994, retaining it for the next four years.

★★

On the Line

There have been no more dramatic Olympic victories than Debbie Flintoff-King's win in the 400 metre hurdles at Los Angeles in 1984. In the final King was behind the field in fifth position as they jumped the eighth hurdle. The Soviet runner, Tatyana Ledovskaya, had moved decisively to the lead, but as they cleared the tenth and last barrier, the superbly fit Flintoff-King caught the world champion Sabine Busch. She still trailed another runner and Ledovskaya. Right on the finish line, Ledovskaya failed to dip into the tape and the fast-finishing King thrust forward and beat her by one hundredth of a second at 53:17, an Olympic record.

One Off

Edward Egan of the United States has been the only athlete to win Gold Medals in both the summer and winter Olympics. He won the light heavyweight boxing championship in 1920 and in 1932 was a member of the winning four-man bobsled team at the winter Olympics.

One-man Club

The fortunes of the Santos Club of Sao Paulo, Brazil were dealt around the brilliance of one man. The club began in 1916 but it discovered the 15-year-old Pelé in 1950. Pelé's brilliance was such that he was a feared figure in World Cup competition and dominated the local league. Santos harvested millions of dollars from whistle-stop match tours around the world, featuring Pelé, rather like basketball's Harlem Globe Trotters. The touring and playing burnt out many young players before they had a chance to establish their talent. Pelé inspired victories in the South American Cup and the World Club Cup in 1962 and 1963. To get away from it all Pelé eventually went to America in 1975, after an 18-month retirement, to play for Cosmos of New York in the North American Soccer League. Here was a one-man league as Pelé's presence lifted the image of soccer through North America to such an extent that the team had won through to the World Cup qualifying round in the last two petitions. So dominant was Pelé in Brazilian football that a manager of the Brazilian team Joao Saldanajz was moved to say: 'Pelé is to Brazilian football is what Shakespeare is to English Literature.' Pelé's game was built on impeccable skills, speed, uncanny anticipation and a marvellous striking of the ball. He scored one of the unforgettable World Cup goals against

Sweden when he was just 17. Pelé was presented with the FIFA gold medal Award 'for outstanding service to the world wide game' in 1982. In 1994 he was appointed Brazil's Minister of Sport.

Open Golf Tournaments

The first British Open golf tournament took place at Prestwick on 17 October 1860. Eight competitors took part and the lowest score over three 12-round holes was recorded by Willie Park. Prestwick hosted the first 12 Opens, and all subsequent championships have been played over seaside links courses. The original prize was a championship belt, but this was won outright by Tom Morrison Jnr in 1870. When the event resumed in 1872 the prize was a silver claret jug, which is still awarded to the champion today. The event was played over 26 holes in 1860 and 1891 and 72 holes thereafter. Willie Park's score for 36 holes in 1874 was 174. The best score of the 36-hole event was by Tom Morrison Jnr, who scored 149 in 1870. The most wins have been six by Harry Vardon from 1896 to 1914 and five to James Braid, John H. Taylor, Peter Thomson of Australia and Tom Watson of the USA.

Our Dawn

Dawn Fraser first learnt to swim at the Balmain Baths when she was four. She left school at the age of 14 to work in a factory as her struggling family had heavy financial commitments. She emerged as an Olympics prospect in 1956 when she won the 110 yards at the Australian Championships. The Olympic 100 metre freestyle was a battle between Dawn and the better-known Lorraine Crapp, the Australian champion and world record-holder. The two teenagers fought to the line with Dawn winning in the world record time of 1:02:0. She was the world record-holder over 100 metres for the next 15 years and won gold at both the Rome and Tokyo Olympics. Dawn was a hero to Australians, who loved her down to earth attitude and her antics but she got into trouble at Tokyo after taking an Olympic flag from the grounds of the Japanese Imperial Palace and being arrested by guards. She was suspended by the Australian Swimming Union for 10 years but after a public outcry the suspension was lifted in May 1968 after three and a half years. In Atlanta in 1966, Dawn was recognised and received a special award as one of the great Olympians of the century.

★★

Perfect Score

Diminutive 14-year-old gymnast Nadia Comaneci of Romania caused a sensation at the 1976 Olympic

Games in Montreal for her performance on the uneven bars when she was awarded the first-ever perfect score of 10.0. She won three gold medals, one silver and one bronze.

Played to Death

Carlton rover Lyle Downs was so keen on football that, after being diagnosed with a heart murmur, he defied a doctor's order and trained with the team. He died of a heart attack on the training track in 1921. Downs played 47 games of league football and was also a star batsman for the Blues in District Cricket.

Rare Honour

Bobby Fulton has the distinction of being named a life member of the Manly Sea Eagles Rugby Union club while still playing for Eastern Suburbs in 1977. The international five-eighths, a brilliant, tenacious competitor, had just captained Manly to a premiership, but his signature with Easts could not be undone. He later made it up to his old club when he coached it to a premiership in 1987. He was made Australian Test coach the following year, and then came back to Manly, to take them to three consecutive grand finals in 1995–1997 — wining in 1996.

Record Breaker

Lorraine Crapp stood in the shadow of her more illustrious swimming compatriot Dawn Fraser, but she held 23 world records and won nine Australian Championships in her career. At the Melbourne Olympics she won the 400 metre freestyle and was a member of the winning relay team. She retired briefly but came back to compete in the 1960 Rome Olympics, but her secret marriage the night before she left for Rome to Doctor Bill Thurlow was treated as a scandal by the Australian press and she bowed out of swimming to work as a receptionist for her physician husband.

Top Scorer

Former Australian captain Allan Border played a record 156 Tests and scored 11,174 runs in Test cricket, creating a new record while maintained a Test average of 50.56.

Saints March In

St Kilda's only football Premiership came in 1966 when 18-year-old forward Barry Breen wobbled a point through the posts to give the Saints a one-point victory over Collingwood.

★★

Seafarer

Jock Sturrock was the first yachtsman to represent Australia at the Olympics when he and Len Felton competed in the Star Class in 1948 Games. Sturrock had a long and varied yachting career, winning well over 400 championship races but he is most remembered for his skippering the challenger *Gretel* in the 1962 America's Cup and also skippering the next challenger *Dame Pattie* in 1967. Sturrock was named Australian of the Year and Australian Yachtsman of the Year in 1962.

Soon Noticed

New Zealander Peter Snell was almost unnoticed when he arrived for the 1960 Olympics in Rome, but he won that 800 metre event in an Olympic record time of 1.46.3. Sports writer Leslie Hobbs described the stocky and muscular Snell as a 'Sherman Tank with Overdrive'. At the next Olympics at Tokyo he arrived as favourite having set world records of 3.54.4 for the mile and 1.44.3 for 800 metres. He set a new Olympic record in winning the 800 in 1.45.1 then topped off a fantastic career by winning the 1500 metres.

Squash Master

Geoff Hunt took up playing squash at the age of 12 when his father Vic took up the game for health reasons. Geoff won his first championship at the age of 15 and the Australian Junior Championship and Victorian State Title the next year. He went on to win every major squash tournament in the world and eight British Opens, six of then consecutive.

Star Material

A good-looking blonde youngster, Murray Rose was a surprise packet at the Melbourne Olympics in 1956. At the age of 17 he won gold medals at both 400 metre freestyle swimming and 1500 metres, and he also took a third gold in the 4 X 200 metre freestyle relay. He came back for the Rome Olympics and took two more gold medals, beating John Konrads in the 400 metre freestyle and again being part of the relay team. He then went to university in America, and also tried to break into films, winning several minor film roles. Back in the pool, he broke a world record in the 1500 metres just before the Tokyo Olympics of 1964, which put pressure on Australian officials to put him in the team. The rules, however, stipulated that each swimmer had to complete in trials in Australia before the Olympics, and Rose refused to do so.

The Gladiators

Norm Provan is remembered as an Australian Test player and a great champion and coach for the St George club, but he had an even wider impact as one of the two mud-coated figures in John O'Gready's famous photograph 'The Gladiators'. No other photo has better captured the spirit and sportsmanship of Rugby League. The impact of the photograph was so great that it was used for the Winfield Cup trophy for NRL winners from 1982 to 1995. The picture was taken after the 1963 Grand Final, one of the 10 St George winning Grand Finals from 1956 to 1965. Both Provan and West's captain, Arthur Summons, are so caked in mud that they have the appearance of bronze statues, as they embrace each other after the match.

The Great Tubby

The illustrious captaincy of Mark 'Tubby' Taylor came to an end on a very high note when he scored 384 not out at Peshewar in the third Test against Pakistan in 1999. Taylor was on that score over night and decided to retire, leaving him on the record Australian Test score of Sir Donald Bradman. Taylor's captaincy had been marked by fine team morale, the building of a victorious squad at a time when the West Indies were at their peak, his strong on-field decision-making and brilliant slip fielding. His reliability as an opening batsman finally faltered, although he had come to the captaincy with over 4000 Test runs on the board. He went through a terrible trough in 1996/97 when he just could not get a score but he persevered to the England series in 1999. He was about to drop himself for the second Test but Australian Dean Jones dropped him in a county match when he had scored only a few runs. Taylor went on to make a decent score. This enabled him to lead the field in the second Test and he broke the drought by scoring a memorable century.

The Immortal Trumper

The great Australian batsman Victor Trumper made his name in grade cricket in 1897 at the age of 20 and playing for Paddington he reeled off the scores of 82, 13, 125, 85, 120 not out, 191 not out, 133 and 162 for an average of 204.2. However his biggest grade cricket innings came in 1903 playing for Paddington against Redfern at the Redfern Oval. He scored 335 in only 180 minutes and members of the nearby bowling club had to stop play to protect themselves as balls kept raining in on them. They watched his thrilling batting while windows were smashed in the surrounding houses. One hit travelled 150 yards and broke a factory window.

★★

The Old Dribbler

Stanley Matthews was the first great footballer of the modern era, playing first with Stoke City, England, in 1932. He was nicknamed the Wizard of Dribble for his magnificent ball skills and concentration, which enabled him to dominate matches. He started with Stoke City and made his debut with England two years later in a win over Wales. After 14 years with Stoke City he was sold to Blackpool and built his place among football legends by inspiring the club's FA Cup Final comeback against Bolton in 1953. He played 84 games for England.

The Record Maker

Larry Lamb is one of Rugby League's greatest players, being the first player to score 100 tries and 1000 points with one club, Canterbury, and creating a record of 347 club games, 88 with his first club Wests. He won a record 15 'Dally M' Player of the Year awards. A NSW State of Origin regular, he only played seven Tests for Australia between 1986 and 1988, and was always a reserve. So the ARL's great try scorer of modern times never had a chance to score a point for his country.

The Tied Test Photo

The countdown to Australia's tied Test with the West Indies in 1960 shows a dramatic collapse in the last minutes to bring about the magnificent result. With one over left, Australia was on 7/227 needing six runs to win. The drama mounted with each delivery. Richie Benaud, 52, and Wallie Grout, 2, fell in the first six balls, as five runs were added. Australia was on 9/232 but the scores were tied and genuine 'rabbits' Ian Meckiff and Lindsay Kline were batting. The batsmen decided they would run for anything on the last ball. Kline hit the ball and the batsmen took off, but Joe Solomon, fielding at mid-wicket, grabbed the ball and, in one of the most sublime moments of cricket history, threw accurately to hit the stumps and have Meckiff out of his crease. The moment was photographed exclusively by Melbourne *Age* photographer Ron Lovitt. He and his fellow press photographers at the match had taken so many pictures in the last over that they suddenly found themselves out of film with no time to reload. Lovitt searched in his camera bag and found an old double dark slide containing two negatives. He slipped the slide into the camera and captured the dismissal of Wallie Grout. He had one negative left with two balls left, and he clicked the shutter as the ball hit the stumps from side on.

★★

True Sportsman

John Landy, who was appointed Governor of Victoria in the year 2001, became the epitome of Australian sportsmanship for his general demeanour and for one particular deed on the running track. Just before the Olympic Games in 1956, Landy was running in a mile race at Melbourne's Olympic Park when fellow contender Ron Clarke fell. Landy considered himself to be at fault and stopped to check on Clarke. He then chased the field to win the race, but the delay may have cost him the world record.

Underdog Wins

Sheer will-power carried swimmer John Sieben to a most unlikely gold medal at the Los Angeles Olympics in 1982. Sieben was not considered a chance in the race, but worked his way into the final, shaving an astonishing two seconds from his personal best time in the heats. He was competing against German champion Michael Gross from West Germany, a holder of two world records and already a two-time gold medallist at the Games. Gross had a hot rival in American Pablo Morales and the two took off, to leave the field in their wake. Sieben fell well back into seventh place at the 100 metre mark, but during the third 50 metres he began to move forward and by the 150 metre mark he was in fourth place, behind Gross, Morales and Venezaulan Raphael Vidal. Sieben reeled them in one by one until finally he beat Gross on the last stroke and took the world record by eleven-tenths of a second.

Unique Triple

Emile Zatopek of Czechoslovakia scored a unique triple at the 1952 Helsinki Games. He first won the 10,000 metres and four days later the 5000 metres. Three days after that he competed the in marathon for the first time in his life and won by 2 minutes 30 seconds, the only person in Olympic history to win all three distance events. Zatopek, an army officer, trained himself for distance running by covering huge distances wearing heavy army boots.

Unstoppable

Greg Louganis of the United States won both the high board and springboard events for the second time at the 1988 Olympics in South Korea despite the fact that he hit his head on the board during the springboard competition.

Wine and Wind

James Hardie came from a leading South Australian wine-producing family but his great love was sailing. He won the World Championship in 505 Dingy class in 1966 and competed in the 1964 and 1968 Olympics. But it was as skipper of two America Cup challenges *Gretel II* and the *Southern Cross* that he became widely known. Known as 'Gentleman Jim', he failed to win the coveted cup but proved a fine ambassador for Australia in dealing with the dramas surrounding the Americas Cup.

Young Leader

Reg Gaznier was Australia's youngest-ever Rugby League captain when he led his country against England in 1962, aged 23. Gaznier was forced to choose between cricket and Rugby League when he appeared likely to play for his state in both sports. He joined the St George club in 1958, and by the end of 1959 was an established member of state and national teams. He toured England in 1959 and 60 and scored three tries in his Test debut. Gaznier was a beautiful runner with a superb change of pace and a strong tackler. He was an all-round footballer in the mould of two greats of earlier times, Dally Messenger and Dave Brown.

Youngest Winner

Marjory Gestring, 13, of the US won the springboard diving at the Berlin Olympics in 1936 to remain the youngest female gold medallist in the history of Summer Olympics. The youngest medallist of any kind was Inga Soreson of Denmark who earned a bronze in the 200 metre breaststroke at just 12 years of age.

Chapter 4

A Cavalcade of Characters

A Big Kid

The great Australian Captain, Warwick Armstrong, known as 'the big ship' slipped away from big time cricket to fulfil a promise to the boys of Mentone, a Melbourne suburb. The crowd of boys and 500 spectators gathered at the Mentone Reserve to witness the match. Armstrong chose two team mates, Bill Tootell, aged eight, and Tom Tootell, aged six, while on the other side were 18 boys ranging in age from six to 15. Armstrong sent the boys in to bat and bowled 36 overs to dismiss the boys for 145. Armstrong's team mates were both out for three runs, but Armstrong batted on alone under the old 'last man standing' convention of park cricket. With his score on 17, 11-year-old Billy Godby put one straight through the Australian captain who was clean bowled for 13. Charlie Smith, skipper of the boys presented Armstrong with a pipe to remember the day by. Armstrong said, 'Thank you, boys, I'll never forget you, nor the happy time we've had together today.'

A Natural

Jane Lock was an outstanding junior golfer in Melbourne, receiving a single figure handicap within one year of taking up the game at the age of 16. In 1971, at the age of 17, she won the first of three successive Australian Junior Championships and in 1975 she won both junior and senior championships. She received the MBE when only 20 while she was still at university completing a science degree. She turned professional in 1980 and had a celebrated head-to-head match with Jan Stevenson during the 1980 Australian Open.

A Real Winner

Jimmy Carruthers was the first world champion boxer to retire without a loss or a draw. A former Olympian, he won the bantamweight title by defeating Vic Toweel in South Africa. He defended his title three times and then retired in 1954. He blotted his reputation when he came back seven years later and was beaten in his only fight. He later became a leading referee.

Accident Prone

Frank Worrall was a champion footballer, a five times Premiership coach in the Victorian Football

League and a Test cricketer but his volatile personality was always getting him into trouble. He had a falling out with players after taking the Carlton Football Club to three successive Premierships and wrote: 'For the sake of the club and for peace and quietness I think I had better resign...' He went to Essendon and coached them to two flags. He was sacked by the Fitzroy cricket team after he led a nine-player strike by the Fitzroy players. He later went to Carlton where he made a record score of 417 not out, the highest score in Australian Club Cricket. After his playing and coaching career Worrall became an influential writer on both sports.

Albert the Great

Albert Thurgood was the great player of the Victorian Football League in its early years. He had a career with Essendon lasting from 1892 to 1906, but it was punctuated by a break with Essendon in the VFA competition and then four years at Fremantle, Western Australia. He was a great goal kicker even though he mainly played in the ruck and half-forward and his tallies of 54 and then 63 in two seasons were phenomenal for his era. He is reputed to have kicked a ball more than 100 yards, the only man thought to have done so.

★★

All-rounder

Laurie Morgan first met Bill Roycroft when they were at the same state school at Flowerdale, north of Melbourne in Victoria. The two rode together in the Rome Olympics and collected gold for Australia in the three-day equestrian event. Morgan had a very versatile sporting career. He played 33 games of VFL with Fitzroy. He won the Victorian Junior Heavyweight title in amateur boxing, was selected in the Victorian rowing eight and represented New South Wales at water polo.

Amazing Gazes

There can be few more impressive father and son combinations than Lindsay Gaze and his son Andrew. Lindsay Gaze was in the men's basketball team for three Olympics and then became coach of the team. His son Andrew competed in Olympics from Los Angeles in 1984 to Sydney 2000. Lindsay Gaze had a promising Australian Rules football career and played at the Melbourne Cricket Ground during the 1956 Olympic Games in an exhibition match. He was introduced to basketball that year by his older brother Barry, and took to the sport so well that he made the Victorian team the following year and captained it in 1960. Andrew made his

Olympic debut at the 1984 Olympic Games in Los Angeles, while his father retired as national coach the following year. At the 1988 Games Andrew scored 193 points to finish second on the list of scorers in the tournament.

Apt Nickname

Geelong captain Bobbie Davis was a speedy half-forward, so beloved of Cats fans that they nicknamed him The Geelong Flyer after the train of the same name. Davis went on to captain and coach the Cats and later became a radio and TV commentator, noted for his wit and knockabout style.

Ball from Hell

Shane Warne had a terribly slow start in Test cricket. In his first Test against India in 1992 he bowled 45 overs for the dismal reward of 1/150. Selectors persevered with the chunky blonde spinner and by the time he got to the first Test against England at Manchester in 1993, he had 31 wickets to his name. It was his first ball against England that probably changed the whole Test series as it completely demoralised England's batting. Veteran Mike Gatting was four not out when Warne bowled that first delivery. It dipped in the air and landed 18 inches outside the leg stump. Gatting saw it as harmless and padded up to it, but the ball fizzed across his portly frame and clipped the off bail. The ball, which had spun about three feet, has since been known as 'the ball from hell'.

Basketball Boomers

The United States basketball team of the 1956 Olympics was so dominant that is scored twice as much as its opponents and won each of its games by at least 30 points.

★★

Basketball Stalwart

Robyn Maher was the key to Australian women's basketball success since her debut for Australian in 1978. She played over 370 games for Australia including six World Championships and four Olympics, from Los Angles to Atlanta. As reward for her efforts, and the build-up of ability in the team, the Australian Opals finally won a bronze medal at Atlanta in 1996 under Maher's captaincy. Maher's dedicated and strong play epitomised the Opals' development. She was tough on the court and played with a desperate intensity to make up for some of the skills that might have been displayed by the smoother players of the women's game. Maher announced her retirement in 1999 at the age of 40, and watched the Opals take a silver medal in the Olympic final against the American team.

★★

Big Mouth

Dick Condon of Collingwood, one of the great players of early football, sealed his fate in a match in 1900 against Melbourne when he was free kicked for tripping. He turned to the umpire Ivo Crapp and said to him, 'Your girl's a bloody whore.' He was rubbed out for life.

★★

Billy Dunk's Scoring Streaks

Australian golfer Billy Dunk was capable of amazing bouts of scoring when his golf game was on song, and he had no better run that in the 1970 North Coast Open Tournament at Coffs Harbour. He had a phenomenal 11 under par after 12 holes with birdie, birdie, par, birdie, birdie, birdie, birdie, birdie, eagle, par, birdie. He then added four more pars before he reverted to reality and bogeyed the last two holes. He still had a nine under par 63.

Bobby the Great

Bobby Charlton had a magnificent career in English football, playing in the FA Cup while at the age of 19 for Manchester United and retiring from the game in 1970, after he had played a record 106 internationals for England. He was a star for England in the World Cup victory in 1966 along with his brother Jackie. He played his first game for Manchester United as a 17-year-old schoolboy.

Bold Manager

German manager Josef Herberger took a bold step in the 1954 World Cup when he fielded the reserve team for a first round match against Hungry. Although the team lost 8-3, Herberger knew that his fresh first team could still reach the later stages and go on to bet Hungary in the final. It did so, winning 3-2.

Boxing Idol

Lionel Rose was born at Jacksons Track near Drouin, Victoria and took up boxing to emulate his idol, twice Australian lightweight champion George Bracken. Rose was amateur lightweight champion and represented Australia at the Toyko Olympics in 1964. He was Australian bantamweight champion from 1966 to 1969 as a professional and became the first Aboriginal Australian to win a World Title when he beat fighting Harada in Toyko. Rose became an almost folk figure, being voted Australian of the Year in 1968. He was offered film roles, performed country and western music and bought a hotel near Melbourne. He later went through personal troubles and his health suffered, but overcame his problems to be a respected figure in the Aboriginal community.

★★

Brotherly Act

In the 1896 Olympics, American brothers John and Sumner Paine became the first siblings to finish first and second in an event when they competed in the military revolver shooting event.

Brown Bomber

Best known of the heavyweights of the early twentieth century was Joe Louis, known as the Brown Bomber. Louis reigned as heavyweight champion for nearly 12 years and defended his title 25 times before retiring undefeated. Among the glamour heavyweights of the century was Rocky Marciano who won the heavyweight title by knocking out 'Jersey Joe' Walcott in 1952. Marciano defended his title six times before retiring in 1956 as the only heavyweight champion never to have lost a professional fight. He was the subject of a film *Somebody Up There Likes Me*. Marciano was succeeded by another black champion, Floyd Patterson, who lost the championship to Sweden's Ingemar Johansson in 1959, but won it back the following year. Sonny Liston won it in 1962 by knocking out Patterson. Liston's association with the underworld and his former criminal record did not help boxing's image. He was beaten by Cassius Clay (later to become Muhammad Ali), the greatest boxer of the century.

Career Cut Short

Freestyle swimmer John Marshall had broken 29 world records and 38 US records in his short swimming career. Marshall appeared in the London Olympics as an inexperienced swimmer, came second in the mile and third in the 440 yards and went to America after accepting a scholarship at Yale University. He was killed in a car accident at 26 years of age.

Channel King

Des Renford did not take up a marathon swimming until he was aged 39, but from 1970 to 1980 he swam the English Channel 19 times and was proclaimed King of the Channel. He was the first person to swim the Channel three times in a season in 1980.

Charming Earl

The Sheffield Shield Competition between States in Victoria, now known as the Pura Milk Cup Competition, had its beginnings when the Earl of Sheffield made a donation of £150 to further Australian cricket. The Earl had organised the English touring team to Australia in 1891 and 1892. The next year the Australasian Cricket Council began the competition.

Close Shave

At the 1956 Olympics, American weightlifter in the bantamweight class, Charles Vinci, found himself 200 grams over the weight limit for his class. A severe haircut allowed him to qualify and he went on to win the gold medal and set a world record.

Dempsey's Biggest Fights

Jack Dempsey had a fantastic fight career, taking the World Heavyweight Championship in 1918 and holding it for seven years before being overtaken by another American boxing hero, Gene Tunney.

Dempsey's most remarkable fight was against Luis Firpo, a gigantic Argentinian known as the 'Wild bull of the pampas'. The fight in 1923 produced a $1 million gate at the Polo Grounds in New York. Dempsey knocked down Firpo seven times in less than two minutes but Firpo then landed a tremendous right, which sent Dempsey flying out of the ring. He landed on a sports writer's typewriter, but was helped back into the ring and managed to finish the round. In the second round, Dempsey knocked Firpo down twice and then knocked him out. After losing his title to Tunney in 1926, Dempsey fought a re-match in 1927 to try and regain his title. The fight produced a $2 million gate at Soldier Field, Chicago, as 104,000 spectators turned out. In the seventh round Dempsey knocked Tunney down and the referee began the count, but Dempsey would not move to the neutral corner and the count was delayed. When Tunney finally got to his feet, it was estimated that he had been on the canvas for 14 or 15 seconds, but he boxed his way through the round and went on to another victory over Dempsey. Dempsey's manager protested, but the protest was rejected and Dempsey announced his retirement from the ring.

★★

Dermie's Debut

Dermott Brereton, aged 18, made a sensational debut for Hawthorn in the VFL semi-final against North Melbourne. 'The Kid', as he was known, took five marks, had 13 kicks, four hand passes and kicked five goals in a preview of an illustrious career.

Dream Team

At the Barcelona Olympics in 1992 men's basketball was opened to all professionals for the first time. The United States Dream Team included Magic Johnson, Michael Jordan, Larry Bird and Charles Barkley. They averaged 117 points in their eight games on the way to the gold medal.

Ever Hungry

Kevin Bartlett created a new world record for games played when he retired in 1986 after 403 league games. The speedy, lightly built Bartlett was nicknamed 'hungry' for his habit for going for the goal instead of passing to team mates, but as he kicked 778 goals in his career, he was probably doing the right thing.

★★

Fabulous Phil

Phil Carmen came across to Collingwood in 1975 as a ready-made football star from South Australia and when he kicked 11 goals in a match he was toasted as the golden boy of the future. He never really settled in his career, however, and had his lowest point when he was outed for 20 weeks for head butting a boundary umpire while playing with his third club, Essendon. Carmen's long history of mercurial play and on-field drama with four clubs came to an end in a final, peaceful year at North Melbourne in 1982.

Fast Emmo

Tennis player Roy Emerson was known for his speed around the court and this was not surprising, as he was a Queensland champion schoolboy sprinter. Emerson played aggressive serve and volley tennis, but had an all-round game which took him to 12 grand slam singles and 16 grand slam double titles, more than any previous player. He turned professional in 1968.

★★

Father of Football

Henry Harrison was known as the father of Australian football and was involved in the formation of the game. He was captain of Richmond in some early games, helped draft the rules in 1866, was a founder of Victorian Football Association and the Victorian Football League. He also captained the Melbourne and Geelong clubs, but finally regarded himself as a Melbourne man. He was said to be as 'old as Melbourne', as he was born on the same day that the Port Phillip District was founded.

First for Women

Melbourne restaurateur and art dealer Beverley Knight became the first female member of a football club board and she was elected to Essendon's board of directors, following in the footsteps of her grandfather Tom Stephens.

Football Always

Jack Hamilton, who started his football life as a player in 1948, joined the VFL as a junior clerk, was promoted to general manager and the went on to be the first chief commissioner of the league. He retired after 38 seasons of football, and was tragically killed in a car accident in 1990.

Football in the Blood

The football legend Jack 'Captain Blood' Dyer was born to the game as he spent his early years in the bush at Yarra Junction. His house bordered on the Yarra Junction Oval and the local team used a room in the house to change in. Young Jack literally grew up in the football dressing room. Dyer's strength and prowess in his heyday was recognised in this statement by Melbourne captain Percy Beames, who told the sporting globe: 'If I had a free will and all of the players in the league to choose from, I'd pick Jack Dyer before I'd consider any other player in the game.'

★★

Glamour Girl

Jan Stephenson from Sydney has been the glamour golfer of the professional circuit,and in her heyday rivalled the fuss that now surrounds tennis player Anna Kournikova. She turned professional in 1972 and based herself in America, where she won some prestigious events. She set a record for the US circuit when she scored 18 under par for the Mary Kay Classic, and she won the 1982 PGA Lady's Championship and the 1983 Lady's Open Championship. Having overcome a tempestuous private life, she is now a respected member of the US circuit and a golf course designer.

Gliding Home

In speed skating, a sport dominated by American and European competitors, Andrew Murtha is an unlikely medallist, but he broke through for a bronze medal in the 5000 metre short track speed skating relay in 1994. The Australian team of Murtha, Steven Bradbury, Kieran Hansen and Richard Nizielski qualified for the Olympics by finishing third in the World Titles. In an upset over more fancied teams they then finished behind Italy and America in the final of the event at Lilehammer in 1994.

★★

Good Pedigree

Essendon captain, champion and Brownlow Medallist James Hird is a third generation Bomber. His grandfather, Alan D. Hird, played 102 games and was later president of the club, while his father Alan Junior had a brief stint in the 1966-67 season. Similarly, present day Richmond player David Bourke is the son of former captain and coach Francis Bourke and the grandson of Frank, a classy forward of the 1940s.

Good Spirits

The three Chappell brothers who played for Australia were the grandsons of another Test player, Victor Richardson, who was a hard-hitting batsman for South Australia from 1918 until his retirement in 1935. Richardson was captain of Australia on a tour of South Africa in 1935/36, and the team was undefeated in five Tests and eight other matches. Richardson was a fine leader of men but liked to bring a bit of fun on tour. On one hot day he allowed the bowlers to have beer with their drinks, despite an official refusal from the dressing room. Richardson went off the field, into the dressing room and emerged with bottles and glasses held aloft on a tray.

Great Service

Judy Patching has been a great servant to athletics, and is a life member of the Australian Olympic Federation. Starting as an athlete with the Geelong Guild and a coach at Melbourne University, he was a chief starter at the 1956 Olympic Games in Melbourne. He was Athletics Manager at the Rome Olympics, Assistant General Manager at the Toyko Olympics and General Manager at Mexico City and Munich as well as being Secretary General of the Oceania National Olympic Committee, a member of the Executive Board of the Association of National Olympic Committees. Patching received the OBE and is also a member of the Order of Australia.

Haley's Comet

Haley Lewis was a phenomenon as a junior swimmer. Her first major success was at the age of 10 when she swam the 100 metres in one minute, four seconds, the fastest junior time recorded. She qualified for the Seoul Olympics, but at the age of 14 she was considered too young to go. She blossomed at the 1990 Commonwealth Games when she won five gold medals.

★★

Head of Footy Tribe

The world-famous anthropologist Sir Baldwin Spencer was elected President of the Victorian Football League in 1919. Sir Baldwin was Professor of Biology at Melbourne University. The VFL position was left vacant after banker O. N. Williams suddenly resigned in 1917. Sir Charles Brownlow, who chaired the meeting when Williams resigned, said he probably had a very good reason and he would not ask him to reconsider the matter. Baldwin Spencer's journeys into outback Australia are now famous. He recorded on film, in still photographs and on wax cylinder records, studies of traditional Aboriginal societies, their language and music. His books are considered classics in the field of anthropology. The connection with football began when he was president of the Melbourne University Sports Union and encouraged the entry of the university team into VFL. With the university's departure in 1914, he began following Carlton. The university's decision to quit the league followed 51 consecutive defeats. Some of its players went to Melbourne, but historians resist the idea that the clubs merged.

★★

Heroic Horsemen

The heroic feats of Bill Roycroft in the Rome Games in 1960 were duplicated at Berlin in 1936 when German army officer Konrad von Wagenheim broke his collarbone during the steeplechase section of the equestrian three-day event. Knowing that his team would be out if he did not finish the course, he remounted his horse and finished the course. The next day he competed in the jumping competition and he fell again. Both horse and rider recovered and finished and the German team was placed first.

Hit Pitcher

Tanya Harding was the key player in the Australian softball team which took a bronze medal in Atlanta in 1996. Harding, from Brisbane, caused a storm in the United States when she pitched UCLA to victory in the USA's College Division One title match. She had only a 10-week stint at UCLA and left soon after the title which lead to suggestions that she was a 'ring in'. Australia kept up its standard when it won the bronze medal at the Sydney Games.

★★

Hugh's Ground

The Melbourne Cricket Ground was definitely Hugh Trumble's ground as he took two hat tricks there with his off spin bowling. The first was In 1901-1902 and the next in 1903-1904, both times against England. Trumble took 140 wickets in 32 Tests and captained Australia, but his association with the Melbourne Cricket Ground lingered on as he became Secretary of the Melbourne Cricket Club in 1911 and served in that position for 27 years.

King of the Road

Mario Andretti holds a unique motor racing double. He is the only driver to have won both the Formula One World Driver's Championship and the Indy Car Championship, which he won four times, in 1965, 1966, 1969 and 1984.

Late Starter

Colin Coates has a remarkable record of having competed in five successive Winter Olympics as a speed skater. At the age of 41 he was selected as coach of the speed skating team for the Games at Calgary in Canada in 1984. He was listed as a competitor, but that was only to boost Australia's squads and numbers on paper allowing them to send more support staff to the Games. He promised Geoff Henke, the team manager, that he wouldn't compete. During the Games Henke watched the 10,000 metre speed skating on television at the Australian Headquarters only to see Coates lined up in the field. Hinke raced to the rink but was too late and Coates had competed. Coates was exhausted after registering an Australian record time. His record is even more remarkable when it is considered that he received no funding and was a sole Australian representative at the Olympics at his first three Games, and one of a two-man team in 1976.

Libba's Winning Way

When Footscray rover Tony Liberatore won the AFL Brownlow Medal in 1990 he created a unique record, having also won the Morrish Medal for best player in the under 19s, and the Gardiner Medal twice for best player in the reserves. Only 164 centimetres, Liberatore is noted for his tackling and has been nicknamed 'the human clamp'.

Long Career

Sam Newman, the controversial star of 'The Footy Show' on Channel 9, ended his career in 1980 after playing 300 games for Geelong. He was seriously hurt early in his football life and had a kidney operation, but returned strongly and became a great team player and captain.

Loud Laurie

Laurie Lawrence is as well known to Australian swimming as many of the top swimmers, as his flamboyant style of coaching has brought him to the public eye. After a successful career in Rugby Union in Queensland, he began coaching swimmers in 1966 and inspired such swimmers as Stephen Holland, Tracey Wickam, John Sieben and Duncan Armstrong, bringing them Olympic and Commonwealth gold medals. His flamboyant style, competitiveness and unashamed patriotism have endeared him to Australian crowds.

★★

Lucky Escape

Wrestler Dick Garrard was lucky to escape with his life when his car smashed into a telegraph pole in Denver, Colarado. He received many broken bones and internal injuries. 'You will never wrestle again,' a doctor told him, but eight months later he successfully defended his Australian title. Known as 'The Mighty Atom', Garrard won the Australian title in 1930 and until his retirement in 1956 he was undefeated in Australia in lightweight and welterweight, freestyle wrestling. From 1931 until 1956 his overall record was 516 wins from 525 bouts. He competed at three Olympic Games and won a silver medal in London in 1948. He also represented Victoria in pistol shooting and surfing.

McGuane's Run

Nick McGuane of Collingwood staged a brilliant solo effort against Carlton in 1994 when he got the ball behind the centre and began a zig-zagging run bouncing the ball seven times, darting and dodging until he got into position to kick a goal. Collingwood won the match.

★★

Musical Walks

Of the great sprint walkers of the early days of the modern Olympics was Ugo Frigerio of Italy who won the 3000 metre walk at Antwerp. Just before the beginning of the race Frigerio approached the conductor of the band in the middle of the field and handed him several pages of sheet music, which he requested to be played during the race. Accompanied by his own background music, Frigerio moved to the front and led the entire race, pausing only once towards the end to conduct the band for a moment. He won easily by 20 metres.

★★

Not Cricket

The great England player Dr W.G. Grace was used to controlling events on the cricket field and got a shock when he faced the Australian fast bowler Ernie Jones at Lords in 1896. Jones's first few balls hit Grace on the body and the fourth went through his beard and on to the boundary. Grace stepped up to Jones with a glare and demanded 'What ever are ye at?' Jones is said to have replied, 'I'm sorry Doctor, she slipped.' Jones, from South Australia, brought a new dimension of ferociousness to Australian cricket, and he was not out of the same mould as the gentlemen of England and Australia. When an English cricketer asked him if he went to Prince Alfred College, he said: 'Oh yes sir, I drive through on a dustcart nearly every day.'

Old Father Time

Former champion Geelong footballer and captain Peter 'The Great' Burns, retired from the game in 1906 at the age of 36, but then spent more than 30 years as time-keeper for the club.

★★

Old Man Football

The oldest man to play league football was Harry Cumberland whose career spanned 30 years. He played for Melbourne and St Kilda before going to Adelaide where he won a Magarey Medal. When he played his last game in 1920 he was 43 years old.

Old Salt

Yachtsman Hubert Raudaschl of Austria became the first person ever to compete in nine Olympics when he came to the 1996 Games at Atlanta. He had been an emergency for the 1960 team.

Place Kick Desperation

The last man to kick a place kick in league football was Fitzroy's Tony Ongarello who, after scoring 11 behinds in a row in a match against Geelong in 1955, resorted to a couple of place kicks in the next match. The hoots of derision from the crowd were silenced when he kicked two perfect goals.

Second String

Maureen Caird was only 17 when she was selected for the Mexico Olympic Games to run in the 80 metre hurdles. She was chosen as a second string to the world record holder Pam Kilborn. In the Olympic final, which was run in the rain, a poor start by Kilborn allowed Caird to take the lead and she flashed through the tape ahead of her team mate. It was the first time she had ever beaten Kilborn over the hurdles.

Seoul Sisters

US sprinter Florence Griffith-Joyner, or Flo-jo as she was called, won three gold medals (100 metres, 200 metres, long jump) and one silver (sprint relay) at the Seoul Olympics, while her sister-in-law Jackie Joyner-Kersee won the heptathlon and the long jump.

Short and Sweet

Willie Anderson was the first great American professional golfer, but he died at the age of 30 of arteriosclerosis, having played three 36 hole matches in a week. Anderson was born in Scotland in 1880 and went to America with his parents at the age of 15. He won the US Open title at the age of 17 and went on to be the first player to win it four times.

Slow Beginner

South Melbourne captain and Brownlow medallist Ron Clegg was idolised by supporters, but he was not noted for his ability to find employment outside the football field. At one point the club arranged for him to start work at a local service station. When Clegg turned up late for work the boss said to him: 'You should have been here at eight o'clock.' Clegg replied: 'Why, what happened?'

★★

Soccer Prodigy

Australian Craig Johnson was the youngest player to represent Middlesborough in an FA Cup tie when he made his first appearance in January 1978. Johnson was born in South Africa but raised in the Lake Macquarie area of New South Wales and learnt his soccer there. He went to England at the age of 15 and played in the FA Cup at the age of 17. He transferred to Liverpool and was a member of the treble winning 1983/1984 side, which won the League Championship, FA Cup and the European Cup. The highlight of his career came when he scored a goal in his team's FA Cup final win over Everton in 1985/86. After playing two more seasons, Johnson retired at the age of 27 and returned to Australia where he focused his attention on his own marketing company and was involved in the administration of local soccer, and the modified soccer game Rooball.

Soccer Start

Charles Perkins, the first Aborigine to head a Federal Government Department, had a fine soccer career in his youth at the Old Telegraph Station at Alice Springs. He moved to Adelaide and played junior soccer with the Port Thistle Club. He went to Europe and played for Budapest and then tried to join the Everton Football Club in England. Failing to do that he became a member of the amateur side Bishop Auckland in England and then returned to Australia to captain the Croatia Soccer Club in South Australia and then the Pan-Hellenic Club in Sydney. Soccer payed for his university arts course, and he began there a career campaigning for black rights and lead the famous freedom ride in New South Wales in the 1960s.

Steamed Up

British walker Don Thompson prepared for the summer heat of the 50,000 metre race at the Rome Olympics in 1960 by exercising in a bathroom filled with heaters and boiling kettles. It paid off when he won the gold medal.

Stormin' Norman

When Greg Norman won his second British Open at Royal St George's Club in 1993, his score of 267 was the lowest in championship history and he was the first champion to shoot four sub par rounds, 66, 68, 69 and 64. The 64 was the lowest final round score by a British Open Champion.

Tea Time for Tommy

Tom Hafey was one of the outstanding Victorian Football League coaches, taking Richmond to four Premierships between 1967 and 1974 and also coaching Geelong, Sydney, and Collingwood. His style was marked by a demand for a direct long kicking and physical style of play and he demanded physical fitness and dedication from his players. Hafey made his mark on coaching in another way as his former players Kevin Sheedy, Mick Malthouse, John Northey, Kevin Bartlett, Frances Bourke and Ian Stewart became league coaches. He is now a respected ABC commentator and noted for his dedication for the development of country football, his physical fitness and his preference of a cup of tea to a beer.

Tent Boxing

Jimmy Sharman had an extraordinary record as professional boxer, winning 83 of his 84 fights. He became nationally famous for Jimmy Sharman's boxing troupe that toured Australia, putting on boxing exhibitions at fairs and agricultural shows. Sharman's fighters would take on all comers in rowdy and lively exhibition matches, but many great fighters came through his ranks including Billy Grime, who held three Australian titles simultaneously, Frank Burns, George Cook and Jack Hassen. Jimmy Sharman Jr continued the shows until stricter medical regulations covering boxing lead to the closure of the business in 1971.

Timely Help

Claire Dennis of Sydney was a young swimming prodigy who was chosen for the Los Angeles Games in 1932 when she was only 15. Before the 200 metre breaststroke final American swimming star Buster Crabb, who later starred as Tarzan and Flash Gordon in Hollywood movies, helped her to improve her start and turn. She won the gold medal with a new Olympic record. At 15 years and five months she was Australia's youngest ever gold medal holder at that time.

Up There Cazaly

The man who inspired football's best known catch-cry 'up there Cazaly' was ruckman Roy Cazaly, who played St Kilda and South Melbourne. The shout arose when he was at South Melbourne playing in the ruck with fellow ruckman Fred 'Skeeter' Fleiter and rover Mark Tandy, known as the terrible trio. Fleiter used to call to Cazaly, 'up there Cazza' and the expression was taken up by the crowd. It became an Australian idiom during World War II as troops went into action, and it was later immortalised in a song. Cazaly was one of 10 children born in South Melbourne in 1893. His father was a champion horseman and physical instructor and he trained Roy and his brothers in a backyard gymnasium. The young Cazaly rowed for South Melbourne and played cricket for Port Melbourne. Cazaly developed a number of theories about physical fitness that would see him play until the age of 34. He said his high leaping was helped by taking a lungful of air as he leapt to give him added elevation. Cazaly was a Carlton supporter but was overlooked by that club and started with St Kilda in 1911 to play 99 games. He crossed to South Melbourne in 1924 and played a further 99 games until 1927. He took a year off in 1925 when he coached Minyip in the Wimmera. He later coached Preston, Camberwell, South Melbourne and

Hawthorn. Crossing to Tasmania he coached Newtown in 1951 and stunned onlookers by playing two 30-minute halves in a veterans' curtain raiser and then running out with the Newtown team for the main game. He was then aged 58.

Wheelchair Archer

New Zealand archer Maroli Fairhall competed in her wheelchair to become the first paraplegic athlete to take part in the Olympic Games.

White Boots

Graeme 'Changa' Langlands was an outstanding Rugby League fullback and centre and had an illust-rious career with St George. As an Australian representative he scored 20 points in Australia's 50-12 rout of Britain in the second Test in 1963/1964. He played 34 Tests as well as being captain-coach of Australian Rugby League teams. Langlands was an outstanding defender and positional player, but he was sometimes accused of being over-confident. He is unfairly remembered for wearing white boots when St George was thrashed by East's 38 to 0 in the 1975 Grand Final.

Winged Keel

Ben Lexcen, originally known as Bob Miller, became a famous designer of yachts and an international celebrity for his revolutionary winged keel, which enabled *Australia II* to win the America's Cup. After a tough childhood, Lexcen virtually educated himself in higher mathematics and hydrodynamics to become a brilliant designer of yachts. He is also a fine sailor and was many times Australian champion in the Soling, the Flying Dutchman class and the 18 foot class. He represented Australia in the 1968 and 1972 Olympics.

Young Dasher

Neil Harvey was one of four brothers who played first-class cricket for Victoria and New South Wales. Harvey went one further than his brothers as he distinguished himself at a young age and was chosen for the 1948 tour of England at the age of 19. He stood out as a dashing left hand batsman, playing in 79 Tests and scoring 6149 runs at an average of 48.42. He was also an outstanding fieldsman. On retirement he served as a Test selector. Robert Harvey, Brownlow Medallist in the AFL and St Kilda champion, is a grandson of Neil Harvey's brother, Merv.

★★

Young Umpire

The youngest field umpire ever in the Victorian Football League was Harry Beitzel, who made his debut at only 21 in 1948. Beitzel went on to become a top umpire and then a popular radio and television commentator.

Chapter 5

Weird Tales from the World of Sport

A Blinder!

Bespectacled Jeff Blethyn kicked 100 goals for Essendon in a season in 1972, the only Essendon player to have emulated John Coleman's feat. Blethyn was blinded after his one hundredth goal as the police horse protecting him slobbered on his glasses.

Aboriginal Curse

When Collingwood president Allan McAlister made some derogatory remarks about Aborigines, he had a curse placed upon him by a Darwin man. The Magpies then lost four out of five rows including three in a row while McAlister apologised to the president of the Aboriginal Advancement League for what he described as a 'slip'.

Back in Business

Rodger Davis's best golf came after he had retired from the game to go into business. The disastrous investment in a Queensland motel project made him come back to the sport and he won the Australian Open, the British match play championship and the Dunhill All Nations Championships in 1986, to set himself up again.

Barassi Shock

Melbourne's favourite son, captain and best player Ron Barassi shocked Demon supporters in 1961 when he accepted the position to captain-coach Carlton. Barassi, who had played 204 games for Melbourne, made the move for a purchase price of £5000.

Barefoot Days

Sam Snead was a poor boy and played his golf barefoot when he was a youngster. He went on to hold the record of 21 major tournament victories.

Basketball's Beginnings

The sports instructor at a Christian Training School at Springfield, Massachusetts was asked by his superior in 1891 to devise a game to occupy the students during the winter. James Naismith tried adapting soccer, la crosse and American football, but they weren't suitable for indoor play. Then he hit upon the idea that a player should not run with the ball, and that goals should be high and horizontal, so that players did not have to try to get the ball past opponents at ground level. He asked a janitor to find him two receptacles for the goals, and the janitor found two peach baskets. Naismith nailed the baskets to the rail of balcony running around the gym, found a soccer ball, and wrote out 13 rules. Basketball had been invented.

Bat on Ball

The broadcasting of cricket began in the 1934 Australian tour of England. One of the early broadcasters was Charles Moses, who later became the head of the ABC. The broadcasters received cable information from England as each over proceeded and they 'described' the match based on this information. To try and give some simulation of actual cricket, they would hit a pencil on a cigar box to simulate the sound of bat on ball.

★★

Bernie's Bad Day

When Bernie Quinlan, former champion took over as coach of ailing Fitzroy in 1995, his team failed to score in the first half of his debut match as an AFL Coach. Fitzroy was swamped by Essendon.

Beyond the Grave

Australian Test Cricket Captain Bill Lawry was never one for fast scoring, but it became too much for one English cricket writer on their 1968 tour of England when he dubbed Lawry 'the corpse with pads on'. In the fifth Test Lawry had ground out 135 runs in seven and a half hours. The innings so enraged former great Keith Miller that he called for the idea of the Ashes to be abandoned. The series was squared when England won the final Test at The Oval with England slow bowler Derrick Underwood snaring the sensational figures of 7/50.

Big Hands

Geelong ruckman Bill Ryan took one of the VFL's greatest marks at the MCG in 1968 against St Kilda, when he stood on Ian Synman's shoulders in a pack to pull down the ball. Ryan had enormous hands and it was said he could hold 38 eggs in both hands. His modern day counterpart is Stuart 'buckets' Leowe, whose hands seem to swallow the football when he marks it.

Boast Backfires

The Australian sprint relay team of Michael Klim, Ian Thorpe, Chris Fydler and Ashley Callus were handed incentives on a platter when the American anchor-man Gary Gall Jr boasted before their race at the 2000 Olympics that the Americans would 'smash the Australians like guitars.' The fired-up Australians snatched victory and then taunted the Americans by playing 'air guitar' on the pool deck.

Born Enemies

There was a problem in the 1958 World Cup when the hostile Arab nations refused to play against Israel. Israel's opponents all withdrew, forcing FIFA to order them to play off against Wales for a finals place.

Bowlers All

Lawn bowls is one of the greatest participation sports in Australia. A survey in 1990 showed that there were around 450,000 men and women bowlers playing. A feature of the bowls calendar is the migration every winter of holidaying bowlers who go to northern New South Wales and southern Queensland to enjoy feature tournaments and events developed for the season.

★★

Bradman's Bad Over

Don Bradman, after facing Aboriginal bowler Eddie Gilbert, said: 'He sent down the fastest bowling I can remember. I unhesitatingly class that short burst faster than anything seen from Larwood or anyone else.' Eddie Gilbert stood only 175 centimetres tall and weighed about 57 kilograms, but he had long arms and a very sinewy frame. Bradman faced him in 1931 when New South Wales played Queensland. The first ball was short and rising and took his cap off his head. The second ball Bradman ducked to avoid – another head-high bumper. The third ball knocked Bradman's bat from his hands. Eddie Gilbert came again and the fourth ball sailed over the wicketkeeper, bounced once and into the sightscreen. On the fifth ball Bradman got his bat to it, trying to hook, and edged an off side catch to keeper Len Waterman. When people said 'bad luck' to him on his return to the pavilion, he said, 'That's the luckiest duck I ever made.' Gilbert played only 23 first-class matches for Queensland, and was plagued by accusations that he threw that ball, and by injuries. He was also somewhat shunned by the other Queensland cricketers. He was a solitary figure off the field, shy and quiet but courteous. His health deteriorated in his 40s and he spent the last 23 years of his life in a state mental institution.

★★

Brick Truck

When Bob Pratt was preparing for the 1935 Grand Final he alighted from a tram in Prahran and was hit by a brick truck. While not badly hurt he missed the Grand Final. The truck driver brought him a packet of cigarettes when he visited his house to apologise.

By Default

Brad Cooper was a reluctant Olympic gold medallist for Australia. He won the medal for the 400 metre freestyle at Munich in 1972 after touching one one-hundredth of a second behind American Rick DeMont in the 400 metre freestyle. A subsequent test found a small amount of the drug ephedrine in DeMont's urine sample. He had been taking the drug as an asthma treatment. This was noted on his Games entry form, but the American team doctors forgot to notify the IOC Medical Commission of the fact and DeMont was disqualified. Cooper says he did not want the medal, but it was his anyway.

Change of Colours

The St Kilda Football Club changed its traditional colours of red, white and black in 1915 because they were the national colours of Germany. It's new colours of yellow, red and black corresponded to those of Belgium, which had been invaded by the Hun and was the object of worldwide sympathy.

Change of Sport

Adair Ferguson was a cross-country running champion for Queensland when she took up rowing at the age of 29. She went on to become a world champion sculler.

Changing Times

The indication that TV mogul Kerry Packer was serious about televising cricket came in 1977 when he won the rights to televise the Australian Tests in England. Packer offered the English Test and County Cricket Board $118,000 for the rights. The Board preferred to stick with the ABC and offered it to them for $120, 000, but the ABC felt that this was too much. Meanwhile Packer had doubled his offer to $236,000, which the TCCB happily accepted. It would not be long before Packer was to upset the world of cricket with his attempts to start his own brand of the game.

Citizen's Arrest

In the unruly days of early football, secretary of Melbourne J.A. Harper stormed onto the ground and grabbed a man who had hit one of Collingwood's players. He handed him over to police on the boundary line.

Close Finish

The 195 kilometre road race at the Tokyo Olympics in 1964 was so close that Sture Pettersson finished only 0.16 of a second behind the winner Mario Anzanin of Italy, but finished in fifty-first place.

Cordner's Galore

In what may be a record, there are 11 Cordners who have played league football, seven of them for the Melbourne Football Club. The original Cordners were Edward and Harry who played for University and for Melbourne. Both brothers were doctors and their careers were cut short by medical duties, but Edward left his stamp on the game with the four Cordner boys who played for Melbourne from the 1940s. Don Cordner, the eldest brother, was a dashing defender who won the 1946 Brownlow Medal and captained the team. He also followed a medical career. Edward was also a doctor and an outstanding footballer for Melbourne from 1941 to 1946, but played only 51 games before concentrating on his career. Denis was an outstanding ruckman who played from 1948 to 1956 and captained the team. He was considered one of the best ruckmen and wet weather players of his time. John Cordner played only six games before he left for England to concentrate on his studies in nuclear science. David Cordner, son of Ted, played in the 1980s for Melbourne and Sydney. He looked like an outstanding prospect when he kicked 117 goals in a season in the under-19s, but his career was ravaged by injury. There were two related Cordners – Larry, who played for Hawthorn, and Allan, who played for Collingwood and Geelong, and three others: E.R. Cordner, who played for Melbourne in 1905 and Jock Cordner, who played for Footscray, Fitzroy and North Melbourne.

★★

Cricket Silliness

When England's Test cricket scores reach 111, the superstition has it that something serious is about to happen, possibly the fall of a wicket. The suggestion by broadcasting commentators is that players and spectators alike should have their feet off the ground at the time that a ball is bowled. It is met with some mirth, and no one is aware of a team unilaterally levitating at this time. Similarly Australian Test players are said to dread the number 87 and believe that batsmen are likely to come to disaster when they reach this number. In fact, to the end of 1997, only 12 Australian batsmen had been given out on 87 and an examination of the records suggests that the number 88 might be more of a worry.

Day Out

Australian Rugby Union fullback Matthew Burke had a 'birthday' in a match against Canada at Brisbane in 1996. Burke created a record of most points in a match, 39, including three tries.

Dead in Tracks

Australian 200 metres hurdler Max Beniton stopped dead before reaching the first hurdle in his heat of the 1976 Montreal Olympics 100 metre hurdles race. Beniton heard what he thought was the recall gun and stood forlornly on the track while the other runners continued.

Down and Out

The worst defeat in National Football League history came in 1940, when the Chicago Bears defeated the Washington Redskins, 75-0. This happened even though Washington had one of the game's greatest – 'Slinging Sammy' Baugh – at quarterback. Baugh threw what looked like a touchdown pass on the first play of the game, but his receiver dropped the ball. Asked if this would have made a difference to the outcome Baugh said: 'Yes, we would have lost 75-7.' Seven years later Baugh played in what is now known as 'Sammy Baugh' day. He passed for 355 yards and six touchdowns as the Redskins beat the ultimate season champions The Chicago Cardinals, 45–21.

Dream Teams

Australian rugby fans dream of a match between the Australian Rugby League team, the Kangaroos and the Australian Rugby Union team, the Wallabies. Such a game would draw a full house at the biggest Sydney stadium. In fact the clash actually happened in four matches in 1909. The Wallabies and Kangaroos shared the series 2/2, all four matches being played under professional Rugby League rules. In the first match the Kangaroos for 29 defeated the Wallabies 26. In the next, the Wallabies, 34, defeated Kangaroos, 21. Then the Wallabies won 15-6 and in the final game the Kangaroos won 8–6. After the match the Wallabies had all agreed to become full time professionals. The fledgling Rugby League movement grew in strength while Rugby Union suffered a serious downturn in popularity.

Dull Days

In one of the dullest Tests in history, in Manchester in 1964, Australian Captain Bob Simpson gave an indication of depths to which the game can plummet when he scored 311 runs in two days and 40 minutes. One Fleet Street newspaper described his effort as 'belonging to the weirder regions of record compiling, like pole-squatting or a coast-to-coast race on stilts.' Australia made 8/656 and England made 611, including two incredible slow innings by Ted Dexter, 174, and Ken Barrington, 256.

Easy Pickings

In 1915 Melbourne Grammar boy J.C. Sharp hit 356 not out in a cricket match against Geelong College while his partner R.W. Herring made 238, in a total of 961. Herring went on to be a World War II general and lieutenant governor of Victoria.

Tedious Cannons

In billiards, before the cradle cannon was outlawed, players could keep the balls close together as they scored their breaks. The highest break under the old method was 499,135 by Tom Reise who played from 3 June to 6 July 1907 before his concentration snapped as he approached the 500,000 mark.

Endless Show Ends

Channel 7's Sunday morning 'World of Sport' ran for 28 years and 1355 episodes before it ended in 1987. The star of the show was Lou Richards, but there were many memorable figures such as Ron Casey, Jack Dyer, Bob Davis and 'Doutta Doug' Elliot.

Enter the Ladies

Women made their first appearance in the modern Olympics in 1900, and Charlotte Cooper of Great Britain became the first champion winning the tennis.

Even John

John Davies played a dangerous game with his style of swimming at an even pace rather than sprinting at the start and hoping for a finishing burst. The breaststroke specialist won a gold medal at Helsinki in 1952 after performing extremely well as a student at Michigan University. In the final he swam the four laps in almost uniform speed and caught, in the last few yards, swimmers who had sprinted early and were at the end of their run. Davies returned to the United States after the Games and his legal career developed, culminating to his appointment as a judge at the US Federal Court in 1986.

Fast Growing

Indoor cricket started in 1978 as a practice program in Western Australia for the outdoor game, but is now developed into one of Australia's most popular sports with nearly half a million participants. The game's rules have been modified and developed to make for very tense and athletic contests between teams of eight players on a netted field about the size of a tennis court.

Fast Man

James 'Cool Papa' Bell was so fast between the bases that a fellow player in the then Negro National League, Satchel Paige, said of him: 'He was so fast that he could turn out the light and be in bed before the room got dark.' He once scored from first base on a sacrifice bunt and in 1945 he was still among the stolen base leaders in his league.

Father's Help

Bruce Devlin took up golf as a boy to help his father recover from a motor accident injury. While working as a plumber in his father's firm, he achieved success as an amateur golfer and became the first amateur for 21 years to win the Australian Open in 1960. He turned professional and by 1966 he had won a share of prize money in 51 successive tournaments, a record sequence.

★★

Feathers Ruffled

Newspaper publisher Ranald McDonald was swept into office as head of the new Magpies in 1982, promising greater efficiency on and off the field. He left in 1986 with the club in debt to the tune of $2.9 million and attendance having dropped by 20%.

Fifth Quarter

A game at Hawthorn in 1960 ran 32 minutes and 33 seconds over time, the equivalent of a fifth quarter. Negative play by Hawthorn's backs against Footscray and the strong south-easterly wind caused the extended time, with the man over the road having more kicks than any of the players.

Five-year Plan

When golden boy Ron Barassi made a second coming to Melbourne as Coach in 1981, he said he had a five-year plan to lead the Demons from the wilderness after 16 bleak years. Melbourne finished twelfth, eighth, eighth, ninth and eleventh before Barassi left with his first real failure in league football.

★★

Free Kicks

In a match between South Melbourne and St Kilda in 1910 there were more free kicks than those gained in the field of play. The umpire awarded 100 free kicks.

Front Page Rage

Peter Norman, a 26-year-old school teacher and Salvation Army officer, had his photograph on page 1 of the world's newspapers when he won a silver medal in the 200 metre sprint at Mexico City in 1968. Standing on the rostrum with Norman were American athletes Tommy Smith and John Carlos, who gave their defiant 'black power' salutes of upraised fists as the American anthem played. Norman, standing between them, wore a peace and unity badge on his tracksuit, but he had no part in the American protest.

Geelong's Quadrella

Geelong had its finest VFL year in 1951 when it finished on top of the ladder and won the Premiership while Bernie Smith won the Brownlow Medal for best and fairest in the VFL and George Goninon topped the goal-kicking list with 86 goals.

★★

Go-cart Start

Wayne Gardner was the first Australian to win the 500CC World Motor Cycling Championship in 1987. As a boy he was devoted to go-carting but he switched to motorcycles after he discovered a broken down mini bike and got it going. He participated in dirt track mini bike racing before going on to racing the big machines.

Goal Feast

It rained goals for AFL full forwards when Essendon met Geelong at the MCG in 1993. Essendon star Paul Salmon was having a dream day and kicked 10.6 in Essendon's win over Geelong, but Gary Abblett, Geelong's champion, kicked a phenomenal 14.7. It was the highest score in a losing side.

Got the Bird

Western Australian batsman John Inverarity was stunned in a Shield Match against South Australia when a ball from Greg Chappell changed direction in mid-flight and hit his stumps. The ball had hit a swallow that flew across the pitch. The bird died instantly and the umpire Col Eagar decided that the ball was dead too so Inverarity continued to make 89.

★★

Hello Adios

Punters wondering why harness racers in Australia and elsewhere carry the prefix name Adios can be happy in the knowledge that they are the progeny of Adios Butler, who won American pacing's triple crown in 1959. He was the first horse ever to break two minutes in the most famous and oldest race, the Little Brown Jug, run at the Delaware County Fair over one mile.

Home Town Decision

When Germany's sprint cyclist Toni Merkens fouled another rider in the sprint cycling final he was not disqualified, but instead fined 100 marks. This allowed him to win the gold medal.

Hudson's Fate

Hawthorn's full forward Peter Hudson had three chances to break Bob Pratt's record of 150 goals in a season in the Grand Final match against St Kilda in 1970. First Hudson kicked the ball through the goals, but the score was disallowed because the umpire had blown time on. Next he kicked a punt straight into the man of the mark, St Kilda's Barry Lawrence. Finally he ran into an open goal and he managed to kick the ball out of bounds.

★★

Huge Crowd

The AFL Grand Final record stands at 127,696 at the Melbourne Cricket Ground when Collingwood was defeated by Carlton in 1970. Despite extensive rebuilding, the ground can no longer hold 100,000 people as seating has reduced the crowd capacity, but an expansion plan announced in 2001 will make 100,000 possible again. The only other Australian stadium with such capacity is Stadium Australia, built for the 2000 Olympics at Homebush, Sydney.

Humour Helps

English cricketer Morris Leyland became a favourite of Australian crowds, even through the tense times of the bodyline tour of Australia. Fielding on the boundary, Leyland had to avoid a cushion thrown at him, and then a dust bomb and an empty beer bottle. Leyland took no notice until a full bottle of beer came sailing over his shoulder. He picked it up and said: 'Now, can anyone lend me an opener?' There was a laugh and openers were offered. He ripped off the top, wished them good health and put the bottle down on the boundary edge saying: 'Look after it for me.' In subsequent matches Leyland was greeted with applause whenever he went out to bat, or took up a fielding position near the boundary. He was offered quite a few drinks as well, but always declined, saying: 'I'll save that for later.'

Impossible Golf

In 1987 the Australian Open Golf Championship had to be postponed for one round when players staged a walk off at the Royal Melbourne Course in the final round. The walk off was caused by a side hill pin placement on the third hole that, accompanied by the stiff wind that had prevailed, made it impossible for players to hold the ball on the green when putting. Players had up to six putts as the ball got near the hole and then rolled back to them.

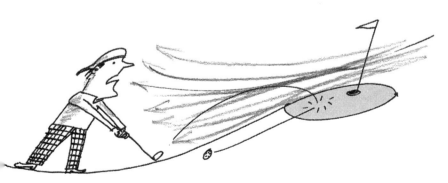

Jumping Giants

Ralph Boston won the Olympic gold medal in 1960 with a long jump of 26 feet, 7¾ inches, breaking a World Record set by Jessie Owens, also a triple gold medallist, 25 years before. Later Boston became the first ever to jump more than 27 feet. His best jump, also a world record, was 27 feet, 5 inches in 1965. All this paled into insignificance when compared to the fantastic leap of Bob Beamon who stunned the sports world when he bettered the world long jump record by 21¾ inches with a leap of 29 feet, 2½ inches in 1968. Beamon made his amazing jump at the Mexico City Olympics, and was no doubt assisted by the high altitude. An erratic jumper, he ran towards the board willing himself not to foul, and then soared through the air at a higher altitude than is usual in long jumpers. He hit the sand with such force that the momentum carried him right out of the pit. Beamon has such a low opinion of his prospects in the event that, the night before his record he did something he had never done before: engaged in sex before a major competition. He then suffered a fit of depression that he carried with him onto the track. As the officials approached him, with incredulous faces, after his jump he said: 'Oh no! What have I done now?' When he learned of his feat he suffered a cataplectic seizure, losing control of all his muscles, and slumped to the ground.

★★

Late Brownlows

In 1989 players who had been beaten on count-backs for the coveted Brownlow Medal were awarded a medal retrospectively. They were Harry Collier of Collingwood, Alan Hopkins of Footscray, Bill Hutchison of Essendon, Des Fothergill of Collingwood, Herbie Matthews of South Melbourne, Col Austen of Hawthorn, Verdon Howell of St Kilda and Noel Teasdale of North Melbourne.

Long Wait

Ulrike Meyfath, aged 16, was the youngest winner of either sex in an individual track and field event, when she won the high jump at the Munich Olympics in 1972. At the Los Angeles Olympics in 1984 she won again, to become the oldest ever winner of that event. Her 1972 jump of 1.92 metres equalled the world record, while the Los Angeles jump was 2.02 and set an Olympic record.

Longest Games

The Olympics of St Louis in the USA in 1904 was staged to coincide with the World Fair. Olympic competitions were spread out over four and a half months and were lost in the chaos of the fair.

★★

Lost to Golf

Graeme Marsh might have been a cricketer like his famous younger brother Rodney, who was wicketkeeper and vice-captain for Australia. Graeme Marsh broke his arm after representing Western Australia in its under-15 team as a batsman. To rebuild the strength in his arm, he turned to golf and developed great skill as a junior. Both Marsh brothers were school teachers before full time sport took over their careers. Rodney Marsh's instructional abilities are now put to good use as the head of the Australian Institute of Sport Cricket Academy.

Lowest Score

St Kilda's score of only one point against Geelong in the final round of 1899 remains the lowest score ever. Geelong kicked 23.24 and Jim McShane kicked 11 goals to be the first player to reach double figures in a league match. Up to that match Geelong had had a shocking year for low scores, scoring only two points in round 14 and 1.2 in the previous match.

Many Falls

South Australian jumps jockey, Les Boots, was so accident-prone that his wife would pack his pyjamas when he went to the track because he was almost certain to finish up in hospital. He was known as the man who had 39 rides and 40 falls. There was the suggestion that the fortieth fall occurred when he fell from a stretcher while being put into an ambulance, but the truth was that he remounted on the horse and was dislodged again.

Medal Treasure

Shirley Strickland won more Olympic track and field medals than any other Australian woman. She finished with seven medals: three gold, one silver and three bronze. Two gold medals came from her 80 metre hurdles win in 1952 and 1956 and she collected her third in the sprint relay team at the 1956 Games. In 2001 she announced that she was selling the medals and other memorabilia so that they could be housed in a suitable collection. The money was to go to various charities and to assist in the education of her grandchildren. In 1975 it was discovered that Shirley Strickland should have won another bronze medal in the 200 metres in London in 1948. A photo finish of the final revealed unequivocally that she finished third ahead of America's Audrey Patterson. The mistake occurred because the judges did not call for the photo finish.

★★

Let's Mingle

A suggestion by a young Australian, John Wang, led to the athletes mingling together at the closing ceremony at the 1956 Olympics at Melbourne. Before that they had marched nation by nation.

Melbourne Boycott

The Melbourne Olympic Games in 1956 were affected by two boycotts. Egypt, Iraq and Lebanon withdrew over the Israeli-led invasion of the Suez Canal and the Netherlands, Spain and Switzerland protested against the Soviet invasion of Hungary by missing the Games.

Ming Steps In

Footscray's champion and favourite son Ted Whitten was left out of a 1951 semi-final team against Essendon because he was a National Service trainee and could not get leave. Such was the publicity about this that Prime Minister Robert Menzies intervened and Whitten was given leave to play. His form in the match was ordinary and when he returned to camp there was a telegram waiting for him from Menzies: 'It was a complete waste of time getting you leave for the final.'

★★

Missing Boy

In the 1900 Games, a mystery remains about the coxed pairs rowing event. The Dutch team chose a small French boy as the coxswain and won the event. The boy joined in the victory ceremony, had his photograph taken and disappeared. His identity has not been traced.

★★

More Money Than Sense

James Bennett Jr was one of America's wealthiest and most eccentric sportsman. The son of the owner of the *New York Herald*, he became the youngest member of the New York yacht club in 1857, at the age of 16. Nine years later he won the first trans-Atlantic yacht race for $60,000 in bets, but lost six crewmen in a violent storm. After discovering polo in England he started the game among his wealthy friends at Newport, Rhode Island. He retaliated for being thrown out of the Reading Club (for persuading a friend to ride into the hallway) by building the Casino Club, whish hosted the US Open tennis championships from 1881 to 1914 and is now the home of the US Tennis Hall of Fame. Bennett created a scandal when he urinated in the fireplace at his fiancée's New Year's party, leading to a broken engagement and a duel with his fiancée's brother. Both men were unscathed but Bennett exiled himself to France. He remained interested in American sport and donated trophies for air racing, auto racing and ballooning, and contributed handsomely to the United States Olympic movement.

★★

Mt Isa Men

Greg Norman, like tennis champion Pat Rafter, was born in the Queensland mining town of Mount Isa. Norman's parents' ancestors are a mixture of Norwegian, Danish, German and English. It is from this background that Norman derives his distinctive Nordic looks.

Nasty Moment

In an ugly incident, Dennis Lillee and Pakistani captain, Javed Miandad, nearly came to blows in mid-pitch in the first Test of 1981/82. Lillee was seen to aim a kick at Miandad and Miandad responded by waving his bat in a threatening manner. Lillee shaped up as umpire Tony Crafter stepped between them. Lillee said later that Miandad had hit him or poked him in the ribs with the bat as he was running a single from Lillee's bowling. Lillee maintains that he turned around and tapped Mandad on the pad with his boot as if to say, 'What do you think you are doing?' Then Mandad responded by waving his bat. The picture was taken and flashed around the world. Lillee was suspended for two limited-over matches for the incident, which most people regarded as a 'slap on the wrist.'

★★

New Name

Constable Bill Proudfoot of Collingwood had a remedy when the police commissioner banned members of the forces from playing league football in 1903. The star ruckman reappeared for the Magpies under the name of Wilson.

New Stadium

The AFL purchased Waverley Park in 1962 to create its own ground, so it could increase its revenue from big games. The ground was abandoned after the season of 1999 when the AFL completed its stadium at Docklands near Melbourne, which was to become known as Colonial Stadium. Originally Waverley was scheduled as an all-purpose ground where big games would be scheduled. Later it became a home ground for Hawthorn and St Kilda, football nomads who had abandoned their traditional home grounds. Members from those clubs eventually became attached to it as a venue. Waverley, however, was looked on with disfavour by supporters through most of its existence. It was said to be a permanent rain shadow and is was called Arctic Park because of the chill winds that seem to blow around the place. The raked back grandstands and the vast playing area gave the impression that the game was going on a long way from the spectators. The general bleakness was not helped by the unfinished appearance of the surrounds, where a blue metal surface created a cheerless platform for the purchasing of pies and other comestibles. Named VFL Park, it had a capacity approaching 70,000, but there was always trouble with traffic and parking. The plan to extend the railway line from Glen Waverley to the ground never eventuated (it is still on the south-eastern suburbs' drawing board) and the journey was made in crowded buses, with opposing supporters chest to chest.

No Pies

When the first Little League games were played in 1985, newspapers reported that pie sales at Princes Park fell by 50% at half time, presumably because the kids who were usually eating them were out kicking the football.

Noble Sacrifice

In 1924 Bill Havens was chosen in the United States rowing eights, but declined in order to stay home with his wife who was expecting their first child. In 1952 that child, Frank Havens, won the gold medal in the Canadian singles 10,000 metre canoeing event.

Not Out

Doctor W. G. Grace, the most famous of English cricketers of the nineteenth century, was very reluctant to leave the wicket when dismissed. He always had some reason to dispute the umpire's decision – that there was a no ball or that he hadn't gone near it with his bat. An Australian, Sammy Woods, bowled him at Lords and Grace reluctantly lumbered towards the pavilion. Woods leaned towards him and drawled, 'I shouldn't go, Doctor, there is still one stump standing'.

On and On and On

George Gath may have had the longest active career in a sport as he drove his first winner in harness racing at the age of 19 in 1927 and drove regularly for the next 52 years before retiring at the age of 71. He won nearly every race going, but was not successful in the two big ones, the Inter Dominion and the Miracle Mile.

Officials Blunder

A weird incident occurred in the swimming at the 1912 Games 100 metres. Three Americans qualified in the second round and were assured they would be in the final. They then left the stadium. The officials then decided there were too many swimmers in the final and they needed semi-finals. They ran these off but forgot to tell the Americans. The next day when the American team members Duke Kahanamoku, Kenneth Huszach and Perry McGillivray arrived, they discovered that they had been eliminated. Through a morning of protest the Americans were allowed to swim in a special race. It was decided that if they surpassed the time of the slowest qualifier in the semi-finals they would be allowed to start in the final. Kahanamoku and Huszach did so and went on to take the gold and bronze medals. Kahanamoku, an Hawaiian who became a surfing icon, was so far ahead in the final that he had time to look back, and then ease up towards the finish.

★★

'Ol' Pete's' Greatest Moment

Champion baseball pitcher Alexander 'Ol' Pete' Grover was dozing in the pits during the seventh game of the World Series in 1926. He was nearing the end of his career and, having pitched and won two complete games, did not expect to be called on again. In fact he was suffering from a fairly habitual hangover, having been out on the town. The St Louis Cardinals, however, were in trouble with the bases loaded and two outs in the seventh innings, leading 3-2. Grover shambled out to face the great New York Yankee hitter Tony Lazzeri and struck him out in four pitches. He retired the next five batters, before walking 'Babe' Ruth with two outs in the ninth. Ruth was thrown out attempting to steal second, and the Cardinals won the series. The strike out of Lazzeri was the most dramatic moment in Grover's career, which ran from 1911 to 1929. His war service had shattered him, leaving him partially deaf, alcoholic and subject to fits. Despite his brilliant pitching he was often in trouble with his club, and his suspension for drinking in 1929 spelled the end.

★★

Old Trundler

Clarrie Grimmett was one of the oldest men to make his debut in Test cricket, being picked for Australia at the age of 34. He took 11/82 in his first match against England and 216 wickets in a 37-test career. Grimmett was tireless in his efforts to improve his bowling and spent hours perfecting his craft by developing variations in spin, including a flipper. He even trained his fox terrier to retrieve balls bowled on a backyard pitch so that he could practise more. He and Bill O'Reilly formed an outstanding spin combination for Australia in the 1930s.

Our Don Bradman

Don Bradman was more than just a famous cricketer. To the public eye he was the most famous man in Australia and an uplifting spirit though the depression years. His deeds and his modesty and good manners captured the heart of Australians. An industry grew around him of mementos like Toby jugs and sporting equipment, placemats and all sorts of household memorabilia. He even got into the business of song-writing. An accomplished pianist, he composed the tune for a song called 'Every Day is a Rainbow Day for Me'. The words were by one Jack Lumsdale.

Overreacted

In the game between Portland and Port Fairy in Victoria in the 1890s, Umpire Threlfall forgot himself, fielded the ball at square leg and threw the wicket down. Amid howls of laughter he was obliged to give his verdict – not out!

Papal Peeping

Even the Pope became a spectator at the 1960 Olympics in Italy, watching the canoeing from the window of his summer residence, Castel Gandolfo on Lake Albano.

Powder Puff Derby

Aeroplane racing is a well established sport in the USA, but the best known of all events run by the Professional Race Pilots Association is the Powder Puff Derby, a cross continent race of 2500 for women pilots only. The race, begun in 1947, follows a different route every year. It attracts many international entrants and is run by the Ninety-Nines, an organisation of women pilots.

★★

Prayers Answered

The great horse trainer Bart Cummings goes to church every morning of Melbourne Cup Day, and had his prayers answered for the tenth time when Saintly won the Melbourne Cup in the 1996.

Prickly Percy

Percy Cerutty was a flamboyant and controversial athletics coach but his record indicates that he was one of the best. Cerutty won the Victorian marathon at the age of 50 and set out to become a running coach. Among those he coached were John Landy, Herb Elliot and Betty Cuthbert. He was a cantankerous character who worked his charges hard, ignoring track running for gruelling work through sand dunes near his training camp at Portsea, Victoria. He believed that success would only come to those who trained beyond the pain barrier.

Radio Waves

One of Australia's great victories against New Zealand in Rugby Union occurred in the first Test at the Sydney Cricket Ground in 1934. Australia was down 11-6 at half time and during the break the players did not leave the ground, but sat in two groups on the field. There was a radio microphone on the field and Australians heard Charles Moses of the ABC and then New Zealand team manager A. J. Geddes telling the people of New Zealand that the game was in the bag. The longer the match went on, they said, the further New Zealand would go ahead. This so annoyed the Australians that they really went after the New Zealanders in the second half – and won 25-11.

Royal Banter

The Queen and royal party watched Fitzroy play Richmond at the MCG in 1970. At a presentation of the players at half time Princess Anne said to Tiger centreman, Bill Barrott: 'I understand there were a couple of punch-ups before we got here. Do you think there will be any more?'

★★

Rugby Before War

Edward 'Weary' Dunlop was an Australian hero for his work with his fellow prisoners on the Burma Thailand Railway during World War II. It is less well known that he played two Rugby Union Tests for Australia against New Zealand and was an exceptionally tough forward. He administered his own medicine after a Test match against New Zealand in 1934. In the dressing room after the match, Dunlop set his 'freshly re-broken nose' by inserting a toothbrush up each nostril. He drank two bottles of beer by way of an anaesthetic.

Run of Outs

Greg Chappell, one of Australia's most successful batsmen in Test cricket, lowered his averages in one desperate period when he scored ducks in five successive international matches. He made 22 and 0 in the third Test against Pakistan in 1982 then ducks in one-day games against Pakistan and the West Indies, 0 and 6 in the first West Indies Test and 12 and 0 in the second Test.

Sailors Only

Probably the most specialised Olympic event of all time was the 100 metre freestyle for sailors held in 1896, a race between Athens and the port of Piraeus. The event was limited to members of the Greek Navy. Many and various running events have been discontinued including the 60 metre sprint, the cross country for individuals and teams, the 3000 metre and three mile team race, the 200 metre hurdles, 1500 metre walk, the 10 mile walk and the 4000 metre steeplechase.

Second Tie

The second tied Test match in history at Madras in 1986 came about when off-spinner Greg Matthews trapped Maninder Singh LBW on the second last ball of the match. The match was set up by a brilliant double century by Dean Jones, who endured 45 degree heat and 60% humidity as he battled against the Indian attack. He kept going despite agonising stomach and leg cramps, repeated vomiting attacks and heat exhaustion. He reached 150 after vomiting for the fifteenth time. Jones was doubled up in agony and told his captain, Allan Border, he could not go on. The skipper replied that he 'would get a real Australian out here, a Queenslander' – as Greg Richie was the next man in. Australia finished with 5/574 while India replied with 397. Australia then declared it 5/170 giving India 347 to win. They were well on track when they were 6/331, but Matthews and fellow spinner Ray Bright carved into the late order batting.

Short Career

Bill James from Kyabram probably had the shortest career in Victorian League Football. He came on to replace the full forward in Richmond's Premiership team in 1920, and had one kick for the winning goal that gained the Premiership. This was his only game as he had an accident while rabbit shooting and was badly wounded in the foot.

Slow Johnny

J. W. H. T. Douglas, the England captain of the 1928 tour of Australia was nicknamed Johnny Won't Hit Today by a barracker in the crowd at the Melbourne Cricket Ground. His slow scoring was such that a member of a Melbourne club bet him that more trains would pass the ground in an hour than Douglas would make runs. The trains won by 23.

Smash Hit

Bob Hawke, a former prime minister of Australia, was quite a cricketer in his young days at Perth and at Oxford University, and he looked the goods as he came out to bat in a social game between the prime minister's staff and the Parliamentary press gallery in 1984. He had moved along to 28 runs and was facing Gary O'Neill of the Melbourne *Herald* when he got a top edge and the ball crashed into his face, smashing his glasses. He fell to the ground with his hands on his face and blood streaming between his fingers as anxious players rushed towards him. Fortunately there was no serious damage after glass fragments were removed. The PM returned with a patch over his eye to receive the Bob Hawke Trophy, a bat-wielding garden gnome with a striking resemblance to the man himself.

Spooky Numbers

Richmond and Collingwood footballer David Cloke wore the number 33, played 333 AFL games and kicked 333 goals.

★★

Squeaky Wheel

Champion Tasmanian footballer Peter Hudson was sought by at least four Melbourne clubs but Hawthorn's secretary Ron Cook was the most persistent as he kept flying to Hobart to see him. Hudson was on holidays in Rosebud, Victoria, and phoned Cook to say he wanted to be left in peace and would not be signing. The next thing he knew Cook was at his door. Hudson said: 'The only way I could get him off my back was to sign, so I did.'

Stockman's Sport

Camp drafting is a specialist horse sport for stockmen, which had its start at the Tenterfield show, New South Wales in 1885. The sport is conducted in association with rodeo meetings and the contest is for riders and their horses to drive a selected beast around a laid out corse. A herd of cattle is held in a suitable area, known as a 'camp', and the horse and rider draft the selected beast and then drive it around the course. Regular camp drafting competitions are held each year in the eastern states. The major events are held at Warwick in Queensland for the Warwick gold Cup and the Risdon Cup.

Strange Happenings

An unusual event in early years of the modern Olympics was the standing jump and in 1900 Ray Ewry of the United States, who had overcome childhood polo, won three championships in one day. Ewry won the standing high jump at three Olympics and the standing triple jump only twice, as it was discontinued after 1904. Another strange event was the stone throw which was conducted only in 1906 at Athens. It was won by Greek Nicolaos Georgantas who threw it 65 feet, 4½ inches, or 19.925 metres. In 1900 the swimming events included an obstacle race, which required the entrants to climb a pole, climb over a row of boats moored in the water and then swim under another row of boats. It was won by Frederick Lane of Australia, who grew up close to the water in Sydney and was familiar with boats. He put his experience to good use by crossing the boats at the narrow stern rather than climbing over the middle like the other contestants. He also won the 200 metre freestyle. There was the plunge for distance, in which the contestants began with a standing dive and then remained motionless for 60 seconds or until their heads broke the surface of the water. The length of their dives was measured. Although it was discontinued at the Olympics, the plunge continued on the American Swimming Association Championship calendar until 1946 and the record holder was Arthur Beaumont who plunged 25.92 metres in 1930. The winning plunge in 1904 was 19.05 metres. There was also an underwater swim in which two points were awarded for each metre and one point for each second that the winner was able to stay under water. While France dominated this event, the Americans were the sole contestants in the plunge for distance.

Swimming Siblings

John and Ilsa Konrads learnt to swim at the migrant camp at Uranquinty in NSW after coming to Australia in 1944 with their father Jenus, a dental surgeon, his wife and their eldest sister Eve. So skilled did they become that when she was 13 Ilsa held two world records while at 15 John held six. John Konrad swam in three Olympics, in Melbourne in 1956, Rome 1960 and Tokyo in 1964 and won gold at Rome in the 1500 metre freestyle. Ilsa swam in the Rome Olympics and won a silver medal in the relay event.

Tall Timber

The tallest man in the VFL in 1952 was Geoff Leek of Essendon at six feet, four and a half inches (192 cm). By the year 2001 the tallest man was 'Spider' Burton of North Melbourne at six feet 11 inches (210 cm).

The Bleeding Obvious!

After extensive analysis of the economic performance of VFL clubs though history, National Bank economists concluded that the richer the club, the more successful it would be on the field.

The Googly

The new type of cricket delivery was invented by Englishman Bernard Bosanquet who discovered the 'wrong-un' or 'googly' ball which was delivered with a leg break action but with a reverse spin so that it broke back to the off. The ball was first known as the 'bosie' after its inventor and he destroyed Australia with it in its tour of England in 1905. He took 8/107 in Australia's second innings in the first Test, giving England victory by 213 runs and leading to an emphatic series victory.

The Gunners

The dominant English club of the 1930s was Arsenal, which won the league five times, and the FA Cup twice. Suddenly everything dried up in the early forties after two more cup wins, and a 17-year hiatus followed before they ended their longest trophy drought by winning the Fairs Cup in 1970. After the jinx was broken Arsenal celebrated the historic league and FA cup double.

The Smallest

The smallest country to attempt to reach the World Cup is Liechtenstein, which has a population of just 27,000. Liechtenstein also made unsuccessful attempts to qualify for the 1998 and 1992 Olympic Games and the 1996 European Championships. All its efforts have been unavailing. After half a century of World Cup endeavour another tiny nation, Luxembourg, has yet to finish better than bottom in any of the 14 qualifying groups it have contested.

★★

The Stymie

In the early days of golf players could lay a stymie on their opponent in match play, putting their ball between the opponent's and the hole and being able to leave it there so that their opponent had difficulty in putting. The stymie was abolished in the 1920s when an Australian champion Ivo Whitton served on the committee that ruled it obsolete. Whitton lost to Len Nettlefold in the 1926 Australian Amateur, when on the final green Nettlefold laid a stymie. In going for the hole Whitton knocked his opponent's ball into the cup. Whitton won the first of his five Australian Opens in 1912 and then his fifth Open shot 72 in a storm to win the match after being eight behind going into the last round. In 1920 at the height of his career his handicap was plus eight – which means that he was expected to par 12 holes and birdie eight.

The Youngest

The youngest player to play VFL football was Collingwood's Keith Bromage at 15 years and 287 days. He was spotted by selectors who watched him marking brilliantly in a post match kick-to-kick amongst spectators. Bromage was 21 days younger than Wells Eicke, the St Kilda champion who made his debut in 1909 at 15 years and 315 days.

Too Good

In an AFL Grand Final played at Waverley Park in 1991, Hawthorn had been derided as an ageing team, but demolished the West Coast. They later wore this slogan on their T-shirts – 'too old, too slow, too good'.

★★

Towel Trick

The quick thinking of Australian tennis captain, Harry 'The Fox' Hopman gained a Davis Cup victory for Australia in 1953. With the tie standing at two rubbers all in Melbourne, Lew Hoad was Australia's hope against American Tony Trabert. Hoad won the first two sets but Trabert fought back to level the match. In the second game of the fifth set, Hoad tripped and fell headlong near Hopman's chair. Hopman helped 19-year-old Hoad to his feet. He threw a towel over Hoad's head and gave him an encouraging push. The gesture broke the ice and caused great amusement in the crowd and Hoad seemed refreshed and determined as he continued the match. He won a string of games to win the match and Ken Rosewall defeated Vic Seixas to clinch the Cup.

Unknown quantity

When champion cyclist Russell Mockridge went to Helsinki in the 1952 Olympic Games he found that his partner in the 200 metre tandem was Lionel Cox, a cyclist he had never met and who had never taken part in a tandem event. A week later the two cycled to a gold medal. The pair had time only for three practice circuits in the velodrome before contesting their first Olympic heat.

Vunibaka Stars

Fiji is a rugby-mad country and, despite its tiny population, can hold its own in world rugby competition. Its quality can be seen in its 1997 victory in the World Cup Sevens tournament, held annually in Hong Kong. Fiji won its seven matches 49-5 on tries. Its star was Marika Vunibaka, who was unemployed at the time and survived on expenses from the Fiji Rugby Union. He scored 12 tries in the tournament, including an amazing four in four minutes against Western Samoa in the semi-final.

Victory Celebration

The relief of Mafeking in the Boer War in 1900 had its repercussion in Melbourne when the Essendon and Collingwood match was moved to Wednesday, a public holiday to celebrate the event. For the record, Essendon had a big win.

War Damage

During World War I only four VFL teams kept going: Carlton, Collingwood, Fitzroy and Richmond. Sometimes in the competition there were players on the field without numbers, giving rise to rumours of unregistered players defecting from clubs who stood out from the competition. There was great controversy over the continuation of a football competition during the war, while action at the front took a tragic and savage toll on young Australians, including many footballers who had signed up. One writer to the *Argus*, who signed herself Judy of Jolimont, said she was distressed to listen to boisterous acclamation of loud-voiced shirkers at the MCG when she had two boys serving at the front. Others argued that if Saturday afternoon football was banned then racing, theatre and even reading of books should be considered out of order. The government line was that sports should be continued as it gave some relief from the stresses of war, which were felt on the home front as well as in action. Patriotic funds were collected at the matches to help the war effort. Rugby League and Rugby Union football also continued in the northern states on the same principle. Geelong and South Melbourne resumed football in 1917 while Essendon and St Kilda came back for the 1918 season. The Melbourne Cricket Ground was visited by Prime Minister Billy

Hughes on the eve of the second conscription referendum in December 1917, in which Hughes argued for the 'yes' side that men should be dragooned into the army. The prime minister received a warm reception from the members, but in the outer the air was thick with stones and bottles. It was a minor scandal in 1917 when the Victorian War Council castigated league clubs for failing to deliver money into its patriotic fund. Clubs had apparently found the expenses involved in fund raising had left nothing for the pot. Collingwood, for instance, only had £40 left from a war collection effort of £664 and Carlton could not raise a copper from £884.

★★

Whipping Boy

St Kilda has always been the whipping boy of the VFL and AFL competition, having racked up 18 wooden spoons by 1955, and played in the finals only five times by 1960. Off the field there have been many committee ructions, and even a players' strike in 1911. On that occasion St Kilda fielded only seven regular senior players and officials scoured the streets for likely starters for the match. Having won only two of its first 100 games it is not surprising that St Kilda spent its early decades with an inferiority complex, but all that changed in 1966 when 17-year-old Barry Breen grabbed the ball on the St Kilda half-forward line and kicked shockingly towards goal. It bounced and wobbled through for a point, but it put St Kilda in front and it held on to win its first Premiership.

Winning Loser

The amazing Doctor Roy Park of University finished the season with a five goal haul to top the goal kicking list for 1913 with 53 goals, even though his side had not won a match. Fitzroy's Jim Freak overtook him in the finals with 56 goals.

Wooden Leg

American gymnast George Eyser won three gold medals, two silver and a bronze at the St Louis Games even though his left leg was made of wood. His leg had been amputated after he was run over by a train.

★★

Women Out

A number of female athletes in the Olympics more than doubled in 1928, when women were finally allowed to compete in gymnastics and track and field. However, when several finalists in the 800 metres collapsed in exhaustion, anti-feminists attacked such feats of endurance. The international athletics association abandoned all races further than 200 metres. The situation remained for another 32 years.

Wrong Song

Zali Steggall won the 1999 slalom skiing World Championships. She was less than impressed as she stood on the victory dais. Instead of playing Advance Australia Fair the organisers played the national anthem of Armenia. Zali Steggall's medal was a highlight in a career in which she also won the bronze medal at the 1998 Winter Olympics at Nagano, Japan. Her brother Zeke was also competing in the World Championships, winning a bronze medal for snow boarding.

Chapter 6

The Wide World of Sport

A Star by Any Name

The great American basketball player Kareem Abdul-Jabbar was born Lew Alcindor but, like Cassius Clay (Muhammad Ali) before him, changed his name after joining the Black Panther movement in 1975. His move came just after he had been traded to the Los Angeles Lakers in 1975 and Los Angeles fans shunned him. He became something of a basketball recluse, avoiding publicity and sports writers, but his remarkable on court presence and playing ability slowly won the fans over, and he became an acclaimed superstar of the NBA. Jabbar ('powerful servant) was seven foot, two inches and 235 pounds, but remarkably fast and agile. He was a college basketball star at UCLA, and was Rookie of the year when he began with NBA in 1969. He played more NBA seasons (20) and more games (1560) than anyone else in NBA history, and when he passed Wilt 'The Stilt' Chamberlain's record career score of 32,429 points the crowd gave him a standing ovation for 10 minutes. His team mates at the Lakers presented him with a Rolls Royce as a retirement present in 1989. By this time he had racked up 38,387 points, had scored a record number of field goals (15,837) and blocked a record 3189 shots.

★★

All-Stars

A feature of American professional sport is the all-star games that are held, usually in mid-season. The baseball, basketball and football all star games attract huge crowds, and a vast television following. The teams are selected are usually chosen from the eastern and western divisions of the country. The first all-star game, in 1933, between teams selected from the American League and the National League, attracted 40,000 fans to Chicago's Comisky Park. Babe Ruth hit a winning home run for the American League.

American Know-how

The Los Angeles Games of 1984 were the first to be staged without government support and provided a model for future games when it turned in a profit of $23 million dollars.

Baseball Hall of Fame

In 1939 the Baseball Hall of Fame was founded at Cooperstown, New York. The date was founded on the myth that one Abner Doubleday had invented baseball at Cooperstown in 1839. The first five

Hall of Famers were Ty Cobb, Walter Johnson, Christy Mathewson, Babe Ruth and Honus Wagner.

Big Flush

Half-time on AFL Grand Final day in Melbourne is something to fear according to the Board of Works, which has its peak time of toilet flushing for the whole year. While there are 100,000 odd at the football, the rest of Melbourne is indoors drinking beer and watching the football on television, with the half time break bringing the expected result.

Colonial Power

The Portuguese investment in African soccer paid off spectacularly as its 1966 World Cup team finished third. It drew its finest players, Eusebio and Mario Coluna, from the colony of Mozambique. The culmination of African football came with the thrilling victory in the 2000 Olympic Games by the team from Cameroon.

Courageous Kay

Kay Cottee took 189 days and 25,000 nautical miles to become the first woman to complete a solo circumnavigation of the globe. She averaged only six hours' sleep a night during her voyage. She battled huge seas as she rounded Cape Horn, and narrowly missed being run down by a fishing vessel as she rounded the Cape of Good Hope. The following year, 1989, she received a Medal of the Order of Australia and was named Australian of the Year.

Crowded Out

Cricket took a dangerous turn in Calcutta in 1969 when six people were killed as they lined up for tickets to the fourth Test in Calcutta. Some 30,000 people waited outside the ground seeking the 8000 tickets available. When latecomers tried to jump the queues there was a wild mêlée that resulted in the six deaths and over 100 injuries.

El Eleman

Alfredo Di Stefano was known as El Eleman (the German) because of his blonde hair, but he was a star of both South American and Spanish Football. A young champion in Argentina with River Plate, he went to the Milionaros Club of Bogota, Colombia. He was spotted on a tour to Spain and signed up with Real Madrid, but rival club Barcelona had sealed a deal with Stefano's old club. A Spanish soccer court had ruled that Stefano should play one season for Madrid and one season for Barcelona. After he started slowly with Barcelona, they sold out their share to Madrid and four days later he scored a hat trick in a 5-0 win against Barcelona. His colourful life continued in 1963 when he was kidnapped and later released unharmed by urban guerillas while on tour with Real Madrid in Venezuala. Stefano's skill was such that a Madrid player said of him 'the greatness of Stefano was that with him in your side, you have two players in every position'. He started his football in 1943, moved to Spain in 1953 and had his final season in 1964.

Evolving Event

A blue ribbon event of early Olympics was the pentathlon, originally conducted in the ancient style with standing long jump and standing distance, but evolving into a long jump, javelin, 200 metre sprint, discus and 1500 metre race. After the first three events, all but the top 12 athletes were eliminated. In the 1920 event in Antwerp a surprising world record of 7.65 metres was set in the long jump by Robert LeGendre of the USA.

★★

Fifth Flag

The super VFL team of the sixties, Melbourne, won its fifth flag in seven years in 1960, matching its old rival Collingwood in Premiership totals but chasing Collingwood's unrivalled four-in-a-row. Melbourne lost to Footscray in 1954 and then won three in a row before being stopped by Collingwood in 1958. It then beat Essendon in 1959 and Collingwood again in 1960.

First Soviets

The Soviet Union competed in the Olympic Games first in 1952 and made its mark, particularly in women's gymnastics. The team competition winners began a streak that would continue for 40 years, until the Soviet Union broke up into separate republics.

First up Crows

The AFL Crows entered the competition in 1991 and made their presence felt at Football Park, Adelaide when they thrashed Hawthorn, 24.11.155 to 9.15.69.

Foreign Legion

When it won the 1933 VFL Premiership Flag, South Melbourne imported 10 players from Western Australia, Tasmania and South Australia to boost its team. The support was helped by chain-store king Archie Crofts' investment in the foreign legion which enabled the depression-strapped players to come to Melbourne to earn some money.

Friendly Rivals

Sebastian Coe and Steve Ovett were desperate athletics rivals at 800 metres and 1500 metres at the Moscow Olympics in 1980 despite belonging to the same team, Great Britain. Coe was favourite in the 800 metres but won the 1500, while Ovett was the 1500 specialist and won the 800. Their rivalry was fanned to a fever pitch by the British press, and both runners met after the 1500 race and declared they were glad it was all over. Coe won the 1500 metres again at the 1984 Los Angeles Olympics.

Golden Bear

Melbourne golf writer Don Lawrence watched a young Jack Nicklaus play at Royal Melbourne and came up with the nickname The Golden Bear for the solidly built blonde-haired American. The name stuck and Nicholas adopted it as the trademark for his golfing career and later business empire. Lawrence never received a cent from this inspirational naming although Nicholas always acknowledged that he was the source. Nicklaus won the Ohio Open when he was 16, and finished second in the US Open as an amateur, when he was 20. He joined the pro-tour in 1962, at the age of 23, and among his wins that year was a victory over the most popular player in America, Arnold Palmer, in a play-off for the US Open. The rivalry between Palmer and Nicklaus dominated US gold for a decade, and The Golden Bear developed his own following, to rival the famous 'Arnie's Army'. As his fame grew Nicklaus also changed his image, losing weight and dressing more stylishly. Nicklaus still plays the US Masters, but his last major win was in that event in 1986, when he shot 65 in the final round.

★★

Great Centenary

The Centenary Test in 1977 was the brainchild of Melbourne Cricket Club president Hans Eberling who had played in one Test for Australia in 1934. He organised the match but also the background planning which involved the bringing of many former Test cricketers to Melbourne to join in the celebrations. Over 200 former Test cricketers were in the stands and they watched a wonderful game at the Melbourne Cricket Ground bathed in sunshine throughout. Both England and Australia had a dismal first innings, but the game warmed up in the second innings and particularly when young David Hookes from South Australia strode in for his first Test. Hookes faced the bowling of Tony Greg. He played the first two balls defensively and then he hit five consecutive fours. Australia sent England in with 463 runs to get, and the hero of the second innings was the great character Derek Randall, who held the innings together with a magnificent 174. England looked threatening, but Dennis Lillee carried the day with a magnificent 5/139 to take his wicket haul from the match to 11. England lost by 45 runs, exactly the same margin as in the first Test in 1877. Another moment of drama in the Centenary Test occurred when Rick McCosker retired hurt in the first innings when a ball from Bob Willis reared up and broke his jaw. With the match still very much alive in the second innings, McCosker decided to help his side. He walked to the crease with his jaw wired and his head swathed in bandages and he managed to hold on for 25 runs in one of the bravest displays ever seen on a cricket field.

Hill Track

The Mount Panorama motor racing circuit at Bathurst, 210 kilometres inland from Sydney, is Australia's oldest surviving road course and has been in use since 1938. Its distinguishing feature is its hillside location, which provides steep climbs and descents and a variety of corners, but also allows for the spectator positions for long and short distance viewing.

Holland's Finest

Ajax of Amsterdam is the most successful club in Holland. It has won its league 26 times since 1900, the European Cup four times, European Cup Winners Cup in 1987 and the EUFA Cup in 1992. Ajax's trademark in modern times has been its 'total football system', which has developed a generation of skilled all-rounders whose versatility allows many changes of position. The style is sometimes described as 'the whirl'.

Home of Racing

Randwick Racecourse held its first meeting in May 1860 and is New South Wales's premier racetrack. It is only five kilometres from central Sydney. It is the headquarters of Australia's first racing body, the Australian Jockey Club. Its biggest crowd was in 1948 when over 93,000 spectators watched the day's racing, but close to 250,000 people attended a mass celebrated by Pope Paul in 1970. In 1992 the Queen bestowed the title Royal Randwick on the course. Major races held there are the AJC Breeders Plate, the Metropolitan, the Doncaster and the Epsom Handicaps, the Sydney Cup, the Queen Elizabeth Stakes, the AJC Derby and the Oaks.

In the Field

While cricket matches were played at Gallipoli, there was one record of a football match played in France in 1917, where the officers were beaten by their NCOs by 50 points. The centre of the ground featured large shell holes with two unexploded bombs at the bottom.

International Caps

The most capped players for soccer internationals have been 150 for Victor Chumpitaz for Peru (1963 and 1982); 120 to Roberto Rivelino of Brazil (1968 to 1979); 119 to Pat Jennings of Northern Ireland (1964 to 1986); 115 to Bjorn Nordqvist of Sweden (1963 to 1978); 112 to Dino Zoff of Italy (1968 to 1983); and 111 to Pele of Brazil (1957 to 1971). The following British players have won 100 caps: Bobbie Moore, 108, (1962 to 1973), Bobbie Charlton, 106, (1958 to 1970), Billy Wright, 105 (1946 to 1959) and Kenny Dalgleish of Scotland, 102 (1971 to 1986).

Liverpool Revival

Of the most successful of English soccer managers was Bill Shankly of Liverpool. He had managed various other Northern Clubs before he took over Liverpool in 1959 when it was a failing club in the Second Division. Shankly's dedication to the development of the club and his dry sense of humour created a new spirit at Liverpool and he brought them league and FA Cup successes in consecutive seasons, laying the foundations for the great club of today.

★★

Long Practice

Victorian Michael Diamond was a little-known competitor from Australia at the Barcelona and Atlanta Olympics, but he had long been practising his trap shooting from the age of eight. In 1989 he won the Australian National Trap Shooting Title and he also won gold and silver medals at the 1998 Commonwealth Games in Kuala Lumpur. Nerves got the better of him in Barcelona but he had learnt from the experience and on the second day at Atlanta he hit 73 of the 75 clay pigeons fired and won the gold medal. At the 2000 Olympics he again won gold, missing only three targets in 150 shots.

★★

Long Road

When Australian cricketers went on their first tour of England in 1878, they had a long journey to get there. They assembled in Melbourne on 2 November 1877 and then travelled to Brisbane where they played a Colonial side and then to Toowoomba to play a provincial side of 22. They then went to Sydney, Newcastle, Maitland and on to South Australia and Victoria before crossing to New Zealand and playing seven matches there. Back in Australia they played another match against a combined New South Wales 11 and after three more matches in Victoria embarked for San Francisco. After a train journey across America they left New York for Liverpool, arriving there on 13 May 1878.

Long Streak

Hungary won the first of seven consecutive gold medals in team sabre fencing in 1928. Between 1928 and 1964 the Hungarian sabre team won 46 straight matches.

Mountain Course

The Banff Springs hotel golf course at Alberta, Canada, is considered one of the finest courses in the country. Its spectacular seventh hole is carved out of the face of a mountain in the Canadian Rockies, which surround the entire course.

New Countries

The fall of the Berlin wall in 1989 and the break-up of the Soviet Union brought independent teams from Estonia, Latvia and Lithuania to the 1992 Olympics at Barcelona, while the remaining ex-Soviet Republics competed as the 'Unified Team'.

Ping Pong

Table tennis was admitted to the Olympics in 1988 at Seoul, South Korea. South Korea and China won all four gold medals. Tennis was reintroduced after an absence of 62 years and Steffi Graf of West Germany capped off her Grand Slam season (all four major titles) by winning Olympic Gold.

Poor Showing

Australian cricket reached a very low condition in 1970 when it lost all four Tests on a tour of South Africa. South Africa won by massive margins as Australian batsmen failed to ignite. The two top batsmen of the tour were both from Geelong, Victoria. Ian Redpath had an average of 47, while Paul Sheahan was next best with 30.88.

Popular Olympic Sports

Taekwando, a martial arts sport from Korea, became popular in Australia in the '90s, having been introduced in previous decades. It sprung to prominence in the 2000 Olympic Games in Sydney when Lauren Burns won the bantamweight competition. Lauren, daughter of pop singer Ronnie Burns, gained headlines for a sport whose beginnings are shrouded in the ancient history of Korea. Trampolining was introduced to the Olympic program in Sydney, and Australian Ji Wallace won a silver medal, and was so ecstatic he hit the headlines as if he had won Gold. The most thrilling of events was the beach volleyball, played at Bondi Beach, where Kerri Pottharst and Natalie Cook held Australia spellbound as they took the final against the Brazilian team.

Portugal's Greatest

Eusebio Da Silva Ferreira, known as Eusebio, was born and brought up in Mozambique, one of Portugal's African colonies. Eusebio was the first African footballer to earn a worldwide reputation although many other fine footballers came from Mozambique to the Portuguese competition. When Eusebio came to Lisbon club Sporting to trial in 1961 he was virtually kidnapped off the aeroplane by Benfica officials and was hidden away until the fuss had died down. He played only a dozen games that year, but so great was his impact that he was playing for Portugal in the same season. In 1962 he scored two magnificent goals as Benfica beat Real Madrid 5-3 in a classic European Cup final in Amsterdam. Three years later he was voted European Footballer of the Year. He was nicknamed 'the new Pele' and the Black Panther and was noted for his magical ball skills and amazing speed. A picture in his honour stands at the entrance of Benfica stadium in Lisbon.

Post-war Team

After World War I, an Australian Infantry Forces team was assembled in England to revive cricket after the conflict. It lost only four out of 34 matches played. The team was at first captained by Captain Charles Kellaway but his behaviour left a little to be desired and he was replaced by the supposably better behaved Lance-Corporal Herbert Collins. Collins later became a popular Australian Test cricket captain. The AIF team fielded six players who later played Test cricket.

Race of the Century

The first well-known thoroughbred racehorse in America was Eclipse, from New York State. In 1823 a race was arranged between Eclipse and a champion of the south, Sir Henry, with each side putting up $20,000. The race was held at the Union Course, Long Island on 27 May before a crowd of 50,000 to 100,000 people. In a time trial event Sir Henry won the first of three four-mile heats in a world record 7.37, but Eclipse won the next two in 7.49 and 8.24.

★★

Rail Strike

A rail strike prevented the Carlton team from getting to Geelong in 1903, and a week later Melbourne had to go by boat to play their match.

Scottish Giants

The two great clubs of the Scottish league that dominated the competition were Celtic and Ranges, both from Glasgow. Celtic largely has a Catholic following while at Rangers the Protestants dominate. The religious background adds to the frightening rivalry between the clubs. Since the Scottish league began in 1888, Rangers have won the league Premiership 48 times, while Celtic has won 35 times. Other clubs to occasionally stand out in the competition are Aberdeen and Dundee. Rivalry between the two Glasgow clubs is perhaps surpassed by that between England and Scotland. Setting aside their club differences all Scots unite in their enmity against England on the soccer pitch. Scotland and England played the world's first international match in 1872 drawing 0–0.

Soccer Goes South

Nineteenth-century English sailors took soccer to South America where the game flourished. The first club, comprising mainly Brazilians but with some Europeans, was established in 1898 in Sao Paulo. The colonisation of Africa by the English, the French, German and Portuguese also led to the rapid spread of football through that continent.

★★

Soccer Tourneys

Famous soccer tournaments are the UAFA Cup for European Clubs, (conducted along the same lines as the Football Association knock out tournament, the FA Cup), the European Cup Winners Cup (for Premiership teams from each European country, the South American championship and the African Nations Cup.

Spain's Finest

The champion soccer club of Spain is Real Madrid. It has been six times champion of Europe, 27 times champion of Spain, 17 times winner of the knockout Spanish Cup, has won the World Club Cup, 2 EUFA Cups and 16 Spanish Cups.

Swim Excitement

Australian swimmer Andrew 'Boy' Charlton caused great excitement among Australian fans when, at the age of 16, he had match races against the great Swede Arne Borg in the 1924 NSW Championships. The Drummoyne baths were jammed with people to watch the races and Charlton did not let them down as he swept past Borg to win the 440 yards by 20 yards in 5:11:8, equalling the world record. It was the greatest defeat ever suffered by Borg, who set 32 world records in his career. Charlton repeated the dose in the Olympic Games in Paris later that year, beating Borg in the mile then winning a bronze medal in the 440 yards behind the original Tarzan Johnnie Weismuller. In the next Olympics in Amsterdam, Charlton won two more silver medals but this time lost the mile to Borg.

Sydney Match

In a effort to promote Australian Rules Football interstate, the league decided to play matches for Premiership points in Sydney. In the first game Fitzroy met Collingwood in 1903 before a crowd of 18,000 people.

Talent Pool

Soccer in the Netherlands suffers from the Dutch domestic competition operating as a talent pool for other European clubs. The Dutch teams of Ajax, PSV and Feyenoord plundered the other Dutch Clubs shamelessly for the best talent and are then themselves plundered by foreign clubs, especially from Spain and Italy. Despite this, Ajax went undefeated in 1995 though its home league season and won the European Cup Winner's Cup for the fourth time.

Tasmanian First

Danny Clarke became the first Tasmanian to win an Olympic medal when he won the silver medal at Munich for the 1000 metre time trial in 1972. He was one of the early starters in the event and then had to wait as rider after rider tried to beat his time. Finally Niels Fredbrok clipped 0.43 seconds from Clarke's time to snatch the gold medal.

That Magic Mile

On 6 May 1954 Roger Bannister, with the help of pace setters Chris Brasher and Chris Chataway, broke the four-minute mile barrier. He later recalled the final lap of the race:

'I felt that the moment of a lifetime had come. The world seemed to stand still or did not exist. The only reality was the next 200 yards of track under my feet. I felt at that moment that it was my chance to do one thing supremely well. I drove on, impelled by a combination of fear and pride. The air I breathed filled me with the spirit of the track where I had run my first race, the noise in my ears was that of the faithful Oxford crowd, those last few seconds seemed never ending. The faint line of the finishing tape stood ahead as a haven of peace after the struggle. The arms of the world were waiting to receive me if only I reach the tape without slackening my speed.'

Between that day and the 1956 Melbourne Olympics nine other runners had broken the four-minute barrier, and six of them were running in the 1500 metre final, John Landy, Brian Hewson, Les Zoltoborio, Ron Delany, Gunnar Nielsen and Itsvan Rozsavolgyi. Bannister, who was in the stands, presented each of his successors with a black silk tie with a monogram of a silver '4' and two gold

'M's, within a gold wreath. The 1500 metres was won by Ron Delany with John Landy third for Australia. After the race Delany appeared to collapse and Landy, ever the concerned sportsman, went over to assist him. Instead he discovered that Delany was doubled over deep in prayer.

★★

The Big Fish

American Zane Grey was a writer of best-selling westerns, but he was also a fanatical big-game fisherman. In a single day's fishing off New Zealand in 1926 Zane Grey and his companion Captain Lawrie Mitchell caught 10 striped marlin of weights ranging from 206 to 272 pounds. Mitchell landed the biggest black marlin on record at that time, 976 pounds. Grey's favourite fishing ground was off Bermagui, New South Wales.

★★

The Doyen

Alan McGilvray is considered the finest of Australian cricket broadcasters. McGilvray was New South Wales captain in the 1930s and became a commentator when broadcasting was in its infancy. His style was informed and showed a great knowledge of the game. He left cricket commentary in 1985 after 50 years, mostly with the Australian Broadcasting Corporation, and wrote a memorable book The Game is not the Same.

The Dynamo

The most famous of Russian soccer clubs is Moscow Dynamo, which became a legend immediately after World War ll when it made a four match British Tour in the winter of 1945. It drew 3-3 with Chelsea, 2-2 with Ranges, thrashed Cardiff 10-0 and beat Arsenal 4-3. Its goal kicker Alexei 'Tiger' Khomich became a national hero. Moscow's great rival in Russian football is its neighbouring club Spartak.

The First Grand National

The most famous steeplechase in the world, the Grand National Steeplechase was originally named the Grand Liverpool Steeple Chase and was run at a course some 10 km from the present site at Aintree. The first race was in 1836, but it moved to Aintree in 1839, and this has remained its permanent home – but for 1918 when it was held at Gatwick. The course takes in 30 fences over two circuits of the track and is about four miles long. The race is gruelling and dangerous with high fences and the famous water jump, which has been the greatest scene of disaster over the years. The most successful horse in this event has been Red Rum, the only horse to win three times, in 1973, 1974 and 1977.

The Football Leagues

Rivalries over the years between the two major USA pro football competitions, the American Football League and the National Football League, came to an end when a merger was completed in 1970. The leagues nearly bankrupted themselves before that in expensive bidding wars for players. A recipient was the Alabama quarterback Joe Namath, who signed up with the AFL's New York Jets for $100,000 and got a $250,000 bonus for his signature. The leagues also fought frantically for TV exposure and sponsorships. The dominant NFL signed an exclusive contract with CBS television in 1964, but then NBC brought the ailing AFL back to life with a $36 million contract. It was time for a truce. The AFL, which had existed in various guises before, was created for the last time by oil millionaire Lamar Hunt in 1959. Failing to buy the Chicago Cardinal franchise, he decided to start his own league with K.S. 'Bud' Adams of Houston and other football power brokers. Hunt created the Dallas Texans, while Adams built the Houston Oilers in the new eight team competition.

The Winners

Italy won the World Cup in soccer in 1934 and again in 1938, but in 1950 it was an all Latin American final in Brazil, with Uruguay beating the home team. West Germany came through in 1954 and then the magic of Brazil and particularly the most famous of soccer players, Pelé, gave Brazil the cup in 1956, 1958 and 1962. England's only World Cup win came in 1966 while Mexico took the Latin American soccer to a new level when it won in 1970. West Germany won in 1974 and then it was Argentina in 1978, Spain 1982, Mexico in 1986, Italy in 1990, Brazil 1994 and France in 1998.

Top Course

Royal Melbourne's composite course was chosen because its 18 holes lie within the confines of the original club enclosure surrounding the clubhouse, avoiding the crossing of roads. It comprises 12 holes from the west course and six from the east course and is regarded as one of the top golf course in the world, ranking with the Augusta National Course in Georgia the old course at St Andrews, Scotland, Pebble Beach and Cypress Point in California. Members of Royal Melbourne get to play the composite course in only one event a year, although some sneak out to cover the legendary 18 holes in the early mornings or late evenings of summer.

Top Spot

The Royal Sydney Golf Club, with its exclusive location at Rose Bay, Sydney, and its fine championship course, is possibly the most distinguished sports club in Australia. The excellent clubhouse and the grass tennis courts and bowling greens create a complex which makes it a social and sporting institution without comparison in the country.

The Worst Scores

The worst scores in the history of the Victorian Football League (AFL) leave the St Kilda football club pretty shame-faced. The Saints scored the three lowest scores: nil goals 1 point against Geelong in 1899, and two 0-2s – against South Melbourne in 1897 and against Geelong (again) in 1899.

Tour de Force

The Tour de France is the greatest cycle race in the world and attracts an audience larger than any sporting event, with more than 10 million watching the annual race. Most are just fleeting spectators, often flocking in their local villages as the riders go through. It was first held in 1903. The successful riders have to cover 4800 kilometres of mixed terrain over the three-week period, including some very gruelling mountain riding. The most wins have been five and this has been achieved by three people, Jacques Anquetil who won in 1957 and again from 1961 to 1964, Eddy Merckx of Belgium who won between 1969 and 1972 and again in 1975 and Bernard Hinault of France who won in 1978 and 1979, 1981 and 82 and again in 1985.

Troubled Genius

Diego Maradona was the world's greatest footballer throughout the 1980s and 1990s, but also one of the most controversial. His real glory days were with Argenton's Juniors and Bocce Juniors. At the age of 22 he was sold to Barellan, Spain, for a world record £3 million but then he was put out of the game for four months after a reckless tackle on him. In 1984 he was sold to Nopal, Italy for a third world record fee, now £5 million. In 1986 he inspired Argentina to victory in the World Cup and was the unanimous choice of Player of the Tournament. English fans still raged over his so-called 'Hand of God' goal in the quarter-final in Mexico City, where he was seen to touch the ball before he struck it home. He then led Nopal to its first Italian League title and the UAFA Cup Final. In 1990, despite injuries, he led Argentina back to the World Cup Final, but they were defeated by West Germany, 1-0. He failed a dope test in 1991 and was banned from soccer for 15 months before making a come back with Seville in Spain. Sacked by Seville he tried a second comeback in Argentina but was banned again after another positive drugs test during the World Cup.

★ ★

Wild Beginnings

Tom Raudonikis showed Rugby League supporters the shape of things to come when he played his first games with Wests, impressing with the way he terrorised his opponents with a fearless brand of competitiveness. He was soon playing State and Test football, and even though he won the Rothmans Medal for best and fairest in 1972, never took a backward step. He is remembered for the game for New South Wales in 1977 when he was left on the bench. He was so incensed at being passed over that when he was brought onto the field he immediately instigated a fight with his opposite number for Queensland, Greg Oliphant, even though Oliphant was being treated for an injury on the sideline! The volatile Raudonikis inspired a victory in that game. Raudonikis captained New South Wales in the original State of Origin match in that state, but his coaching after retirement took him to Brisbane. He made a triumphant return to coach Wests, and became New South Wales coach from 1997 to 1999.

War Games

After Germany staged the 1936 Games, its World War II ally Japan was awarded the 1940 Olympics, but they were abandoned when Japan invaded

China and became involved in a major war. The Games were reassigned to Helsinki, Finland, but then when Soviet troops invaded that country, the Olympics were cancelled altogether. The first post-war Olympics, the 1948 Games, were held in London after having been scheduled for that city in 1944. Helsinki got its chance in 1952.

World Cup Soccer

The first World Cup competition took place in the 1930s as a brainchild of the World Governing Body, FIFA, which was established in 1894. The first championship took place in Uruguay, but there was a limited European response, with only France, Belgium, Yugoslavia and Romania making the long journey. Only 13 teams competed, with Uruguay, Argentina, Brazil and the USA the most fancied nations. Uruguay played the final against Argentina and it was a home country victory. The World Cup was held in Italy in 1934, France in 1938 and after the war in Brazil in 1950. It has been held every four years since then and has been developed into an event to rival the Olympic Games in complexity and prestige. To qualify for the World Cup, many countries play about a dozen matches. In the modern version of the game, there are 48 qualifying teams, which are split into six groups. Teams in these groups must play on for the right to enter the second phase of the competition and then the quarter-finals, semi-finals and final. The World Cup attracts spectacular support, with saturation television coverage being beamed around the world.

World Cup Cricket

Limited overs cricket came into its own in 1975 when the first World Cup was played in England. The final was played between Australia and the West Indies and a fine century by West Indies captain, Clive Lloyd, carried the Windies to victory. Johnson eventually lost his title to Jess Willard in Havana, Cuba, in 1915.

Conversion Tables

Imperial measurements have been retained in stories set in pre-metric times. In the interests of greater readability, it was decided *not* to add metric equivalents in brackets. These can be calculated from the tables below. Money values are theoretical only, and do not take inflationary factors into consideration.

One inch = 2.45 cm
One foot = 30.5 cm
One yard = 0.914 m
One mile = 1.61 km

One ounce = 28.3 g
One pound = 454 g
One stone = 6.35 kg
One ton = 1.02 t

One penny = 1 cent
One shilling = 10 cents
One pound = $2